# CENTRAL AND EAST AFRICA

EXPLORATION OF AFRICA: THE EMERGING NATIONS

# CENTRAL AND EAST AFRICA

## 1880 TO THE PRESENT: FROM COLONIALISM TO CIVIL WAR

DANIEL E. HARMON

INTRODUCTORY ESSAY BY
Dr. Richard E. Leakey
Chairman, Wildlife Clubs
of Kenya Association
✝
AFTERWORD BY
Deirdre Shields

**CHELSEA HOUSE PUBLISHERS**
**Philadelphia**
In association with Covos Day Books, South Africa

# CHELSEA HOUSE PUBLISHERS

EDITOR IN CHIEF  Sally Cheney
PRODUCTION MANAGER  Kim Shinners
ART DIRECTOR  Sara Davis
ASSOCIATE ART DIRECTOR  Takeshi Takahashi
SERIES DESIGNER  Keith Trego
COVER DESIGN  Emiliano Begnardi

The Chelsea House World Wide Web address is http://www.chelseahouse.com

First Printing

1 3 5 7 9 8 6 4 2

---

---

Library of Congress Cataloging-in-Publication Data

Harmon, Daniel E.
   Central and East Africa: 1880 to the present: from colonialism to civil war / Daniel E.
Harmon; introductory essay by Richard E. Leakey; afterword by Deirde Shields.
      p. cm.— (Exploration of Africa, the emerging nations)
   Includes bibliographical references and index.
   Contents: The Dark Continent / Richard E. Leakey—An untamed land—Creating the
Colonies—Wide-eyed Westerners take stock—Moving toward independence—Central and
East Africa since independence—A restless region—World without end / Dierdre Shields.
   ISBN 0-7910-5743-7 (alk. paper)
   1. Africa, Central—History—Juvenile literature. Africa, East—History—Juvenile
literature. [1. Africa, Central—History. 2. Africa, East—History.] I. Title. II. Series.
DT352.7 .H37 2001
967'.03—dc21
                                                              2001047599

---

The photographs in this book are from the Royal Geographical Society Picture Library. Most are being published for the first time.

The Royal Geographical Society Picture Library provides an unrivaled source of over half a million images of peoples and landscapes from around the globe. Photographs date from the 1840s onwards on a variety of subjects including the British Colonial Empire, deserts, exploration, indigenous peoples, landscapes, remote destinations, and travel.

Photography, beginning with the daguerreotype in 1839, is only marginally younger than the Society, which encouraged its explorers to use the new medium from its earliest days. From the remarkable mid-19th century black-and-white photographs to color transparencies of the late 20th century, the focus of the collection is not the generic stock shot but the portrayal of man's resilience, adaptability, and mobility in remote parts of the world.

In organizing this project, we have incurred many debts of gratitude. Our first, though, is to the professional staff of the Picture Library for their generous assistance, especially to Joanna Scadden, Picture Library Manager.

# CONTENTS

THE DARK CONTINENT *Dr. Richard E. Leakey*          7

INTRODUCTION          15

1   AN UNTAMED LAND          19

2   CREATING THE COLONIES          49

3   WIDE-EYED WESTERNERS TAKE STOCK          69

4   MOVING TOWARD INDEPENDENCE          87

5   LIFE AFTER INDEPENDENCE          97

6   A RESTLESS REGION          119

WORLD WITHOUT END *Deirdre Shields*          128

CHRONOLOGY          134

GLOSSARY          135

FURTHER READING          137

INDEX          138

# Exploration of Africa: The Emerging Nations

Angola

Central and East Africa

The Congo

Egypt

Ethiopia

Nigeria

North Africa

South Africa

Southeast Africa

Sudan

West Africa

# THE DARK CONTINENT

DR. RICHARD E. LEAKEY

THE CONCEPT OF AFRICAN exploration has been greatly influenced by the hero status given to the European adventurers and missionaries who went off to Africa in the last century. Their travels and travails were certainly extraordinary and nobody can help but be impressed by the tremendous physical and intellectual courage that was so much a characteristic of people such as Livingstone, Stanley, Speke, and Baker, to name just a few. The challenges and rewards that Africa offered, both in terms of commerce and also "saved souls," inspired people to take incredible risks and endure personal suffering to a degree that was probably unique to the exploration of Africa.

I myself was fortunate enough to have had the opportunity to organize one or two minor expeditions to remote spots in Africa where there were no roads or airfields and marching with porters and/or camels was the best option at the time. I have also had the thrill of being with people untouched and often unmoved by contact with Western or other technologically based cultures, and these experiences remain for me amongst the most exciting and salutary of my life. With the contemporary revolution in technology, there will be few if any such opportunities again. Indeed I often find myself slightly saddened by the realization that were life ever discovered on another planet, exploration would doubtless be done by remote sensing and making full use of artificial, digital intelligence. At least it is unlikely to be in my lifetime and this is a relief!

# CENTRAL AND EAST AFRICA

Notwithstanding all of this, I believe that the age of exploration and discovery in Africa is far from over. The future offers incredible opportunities for new discoveries that will push back the frontiers of knowledge. This endeavor will of course not involve exotic and arduous journeys into malaria-infested tropical swamps, but it will certainly require dedication, team work, public support, and a conviction that the rewards to be gained will more than justify the efforts and investment.

## EARLY EXPLORERS

Many of us were raised and educated at school with the belief that Africa, the so-called Dark Continent, was actually discovered by early European travelers and explorers. The date of this "discovery" is difficult to establish, and anyway a distinction has always had to be drawn between northern Africa and the vast area south of the Sahara. The Romans certainly had information about the continent's interior as did others such as the Greeks. A diverse range of traders ventured down both the west coast and the east coast from at least the ninth century, and by the tenth century Islam had taken root in a number of new towns and settlements established by Persian and Arab interests along the eastern tropical shores. Trans-African trade was probably under way well before this time, perhaps partly stimulated by external interests.

Close to the beginning of the first millennium, early Christians were establishing the Coptic church in the ancient kingdom of Ethiopia and at other coastal settlements along Africa's northern Mediterranean coast. Along the west coast of Africa, European trade in gold, ivory, and people was well established by the sixteenth century. Several hundred years later, early in the 19th century, the systematic penetration and geographical exploration of Africa was undertaken by Europeans seeking geographical knowledge and territory and looking for opportunities not only for commerce but for the chance to spread the Gospel. The extraordinary narratives of some of the journeys of early European travelers and adventurers in Africa are a vivid reminder of just how recently Africa has become embroiled in the power struggles and vested interests of non-Africans.

# THE DARK CONTINENT

## AFRICA'S GIFT TO THE WORLD

My own preoccupation over the past thirty years has been to study human prehistory, and from this perspective it is very clear that Africa was never "discovered" in the sense in which so many people have been and, perhaps, still are being taught. Rather, it was Africans themselves who found that there was a world beyond their shores.

Prior to about two million years ago, the only humans or proto-humans in existence were confined to Africa; as yet, the remaining world had not been exposed to this strange mammalian species, which in time came to dominate the entire planet. It is no trivial matter to recognize the cultural implications that arise from this entirely different perspective of Africa and its relationship to the rest of humanity.

How many of the world's population grow up knowing that it was in fact African people who first moved and settled in southern Europe and Central Asia and migrated to the Far East? How many know that Africa's principal contribution to the world is in fact humanity itself? These concepts are quite different from the notion that Africa was only "discovered" in the past few hundred years and will surely change the commonly held idea that somehow Africa is a "laggard," late to come onto the world stage.

It could be argued that our early human forebears—the *Homo erectus* who moved out of Africa—have little or no bearing on the contemporary world and its problems. I disagree and believe that the often pejorative thoughts that are associated with the Dark Continent and dark skins, as well as with the general sense that Africans are somehow outside the mainstream of human achievement, would be entirely negated by the full acceptance of a universal African heritage for all of humanity. This, after all, is the truth that has now been firmly established by scientific inquiry.

The study of human origins and prehistory will surely continue to be important in a number of regions of Africa and this research must continue to rank high on the list of relevant ongoing exploration and discovery. There is still much to be learned about the early stages of human development, and the age of the "first humans"—the first bipedal apes—has not been firmly established. The current hypothesis is that prior to five million years ago there were no bipeds, and this would mean that humankind is only five million years old. Beyond Africa, there were no humans until just two million years ago, and this is a consideration that political leaders and people as a whole need to bear in mind.

## RECENT HISTORY

When it comes to the relatively recent history of Africa's contemporary people, there is still considerable ignorance. The evidence suggests that there were major migrations of people within the continent during the past 5,000 years, and the impact of the introduction of domestic stock must have been quite considerable on the way of life of many of Africa's people. Early settlements and the beginnings of nation states are, as yet, poorly researched and recorded. Although archaeological studies have been undertaken in Africa for well over a hundred years, there remain more questions than answers.

One question of universal interest concerns the origin and inspiration for the civilization of early Egypt. The Nile has, of course, offered opportunities for contacts between the heart of Africa and the Mediterranean seacoast, but very little is known about human settlement and civilization in the upper reaches of the Blue and White Nile between 4,000 and 10,000 years ago. We do know that the present Sahara Desert is only about 10,000 years old; before this Central Africa was wetter and more fertile, and research findings have shown that it was only during the past 10,000 years that Lake Turkana in the northern Kenya was isolated from the Nile system. When connected, it would have been an excellent connection between the heartland of the continent and the Mediterranean.

Another question focuses on the extensive stone-walled villages and towns in Southern Africa. The Great Zimbabwe is but one of thousands of standing monuments in East, Central, and Southern Africa that attest to considerable human endeavor in Africa long before contact with Europe or Arabia. The Neolithic period and Iron Age still offer very great opportunities for exploration and discovery.

As an example of the importance of history, let us look at the modern South Africa where a visitor might still be struck by the not-too-subtle representation of a past that, until a few years ago, only "began" with the arrival of Dutch settlers some 400 years back. There are, of course, many pre-Dutch sites, including extensive fortified towns where kingdoms and nation states had thrived hundreds of years before contact with Europe; but this evidence has been poorly documented and even more poorly portrayed.

Few need to be reminded of the sparseness of Africa's precolonial written history. There are countless cultures and historical narratives that have been recorded only as oral history and legend. As postcolonial Africa further consolidates itself, history must be reviewed and deepened to incorporate the realities of precolonial human settlement as well as foreign contact. Africa's identity and self-respect is closely linked to this.

One of the great tragedies is that African history was of little interest to the early European travelers who were in a hurry and had no brief to document the details of the people they came across during their travels. In the basements of countless European museums, there are stacked shelves of African "curios"—objects taken from the people but seldom documented in terms of the objects' use, customs, and history.

There is surely an opportunity here for contemporary scholars to do something. While much of Africa's precolonial past has been obscured by the slave trade, colonialism, evangelism, and modernization, there remains an opportunity, at least in some parts of the continent, to record what still exists. This has to be one of the most vital frontiers for African exploration and discovery as we approach the end of this millennium. Some of the work will require trips to the field, but great gains could be achieved by a systematic and coordinated effort to record the inventories of European museums and archives. The Royal Geographical Society could well play a leading role in this chapter of African exploration. The compilation of a central data bank on what is known and what exists would, if based on a coordinated initiative to record the customs and social organization of Africa's remaining indigenous peoples, be a huge contribution to the heritage of humankind.

## MEDICINES AND FOODS

On the African continent itself, there remain countless other areas for exploration and discovery. Such endeavors will be achieved without the fanfare of great expeditions and high adventure as was the case during the last century and they should, as far as possible, involve exploration and discovery of African frontiers by Africans themselves. These frontiers are not geographic: they are boundaries of knowledge in the sphere of Africa's home-grown cultures and natural world.

Indigenous knowledge is a very poorly documented subject in many parts of the world, and Africa is a prime example of a continent where centuries of accumulated local knowledge is rapidly disappearing in the face of modernization. I believe, for example, that there is much to be learned about the use of wild African plants for both medicinal and nutritional purposes. Such knowledge, kept to a large extent as the experience and memory of elders in various indigenous communities, could potentially have far-reaching benefits for Africa and for humanity as a whole.

The importance of new remedies based on age-old medicines cannot be underestimated. Over the past two decades, international companies have begun to take note and to exploit certain African plants for pharmacological preparations. All too often, Africa has not been the beneficiary of these "discoveries," which are, in most instances, nothing more than the refinement and improvement of traditional African medicine. The opportunities for exploration and discovery in this area are immense and will have assured economic return on investment. One can only hope that such work will be in partnership with the people of Africa and not at the expense of the continent's best interests.

Within the same context, there is much to be learned about the traditional knowledge of the thousands of plants that have been utilized by different African communities for food. The contemporary world has become almost entirely dependent, in terms of staple foods, on the cultivation of only six principal plants: corn, wheat, rice, yams, potatoes, and bananas. This cannot be a secure basis to guarantee the food requirements of more than five billion people.

Many traditional food plants in Africa are drought resistant and might well offer new alternatives for large-scale agricultural development in the years to come. Crucial to this development is finding out what African people used before exotics were introduced. In some rural areas of the continent, it is still possible to learn about much of this by talking to the older generation. It is certainly a great shame that some of the early European travelers in Africa were ill equipped to study and record details of diet and traditional plant use, but I am sure that, although it is late, it is not too late. The compilation of a pan-African database on what is known about the use of the continent's plant resources is a vital matter requiring action.

## VANISHING SPECIES

In the same spirit, there is as yet a very incomplete inventory of the continent's other species. The inevitable trend of bringing land into productive management is resulting in the loss of unknown but undoubtedly large numbers of species. This genetic resource may be invaluable to the future of Africa and indeed humankind, and there really is a need for coordinated efforts to record and understand the continent's biodiversity.

In recent years important advances have been made in the study of tropical ecosystems in Central and South America, and I am sure that similar endeavors in Africa would be rewarding. At present, Africa's semi-arid and highland ecosystems are better understood than the more diverse and complex lowland forests, which are themselves under particular threat from loggers and farmers. The challenges of exploring the biodiversity of the upper canopy in the tropical forests, using the same techniques that are now used in Central American forests, are fantastic and might also lead to eco-tourist developments for these areas in the future.

It is indeed an irony that huge amounts of money are being spent by the advanced nations in an effort to discover life beyond our own planet, while at the same time nobody on this planet knows the extent and variety of life here at home. The tropics are especially relevant in this regard and one can only hope that Africa will become the focus of renewed efforts of research on biodiversity and tropical ecology.

## AN AFROCENTRIC VIEW

Overall, the history of Africa has been presented from an entirely Eurocentric or even Caucasocentric perspective, and until recently this has not been adequately reviewed. The penetration of Africa, especially during the last century, was important in its own way; but today the realities of African history, art, culture, and politics are better known. The time has come to regard African history in terms of what has happened in Africa itself, rather than simply in terms of what non-African individuals did when they first traveled to the continent.

# INTRODUCTION

**M**any Americans don't remember the executive jet plane crash at Kigali, Rwanda, on April 6, 1994—if they ever heard the news at all. Unlike commercial airline disasters that claim hundreds of lives and hold the public gruesomely transfixed, the Kigali crash killed just twelve. And it happened far away in the Third World.

Two of the victims, though, were international dignitaries. In fact, both were heads of state. Cyprien Ntaryamira had been elected president of neighboring Burundi just

**Tutsi, Lake Tanganyika, c. 1921** *Tutsi tradition teaches that the Rwandan kingdom began with the advent of civilization. However, anthropologists date this nuclear kingdom in central Africa back to the sixteenth century.*

*From 1894 to 1918, Rwanda, along with Burundi, was part of German East Africa. After World War I (1914–1918), the League of Nations joined Rwanda and Burundi into the Territory of Ruanda-Urundi. This territory was administered by Belgium (1919–1962). The Tutsi, a Bantu-speaking people, formed the traditional aristocratic minority in both countries. By tradition, they are a cattle-keeping people. Originally, the Tutsi tended to be taller than the Hutu majority. Over the centuries, the two groups developed a common language and culture. Alas, anarchy and mass killings in the 1990s have devastated these two peoples.*

three months earlier. Juvénal Habyarimana had ruled Rwanda for twenty-one years. They were returning together from a summit of East African leaders in Tanzania. They were returning to two small nations racked by *ethnic* unrest and violence.

To this day, mystery, suspicion, sensational charges, denials, and countercharges enshroud the tragedy. Initial reports were that the airplane crashed accidentally during a nighttime landing at the Kigali airport. A far more chilling reality quickly became apparent: the descending plane was hit by a surface-to-air missile, probably fired from a nearby hillside.

All fatal plane crashes cause shock and grief. This one ignited civil war in both countries. Death squads killed political leaders and government officials, including Rwandan Prime Minister Agathe Uwilingiyimana. United Nations guards seemed powerless to lend protection. People seeking refuge were abandoned; some were brutalized and killed by the Rwandan army and rampaging factions of armed civilians. At the root of the fighting was age-old hatred between two ethnic groups: the majority Hutu and the minority Tutsi peoples.

It was only the beginning. By the end of the year, more than half a million Rwandan citizens had been slaughtered. More than a million others had fled across the western border into the jungles of Zaire. The country's schools were closed indefinitely. Its court system shut down. Martial law was the only law, and no one could feel safe.

Hutu and Tutsi forces also clashed in Burundi. Eventually, almost a quarter of a million people were killed in that country. Although the violence ultimately lessened, it has continued to simmer in both Rwanda and Burundi into the twenty-first century.

Unhappily, those nations' tragedies are not unique. On a continent fraught with strife during its forty years of independence from European colonialism, East-Central Africa has been a particularly unsettled region. Kenya has seen political persecution and bombings. Tanzania and Uganda have waged a full-scale war against each other. *Anarchy* and violence have paralyzed Somalia for the past decade.

How did the new nations arrive at this crisis? Does the strife stem in part from some seventy years of rulership by European colonial governments? Or did the colonial administrations serve to keep a lid temporarily on the ethnic hatred that has been building for centuries?

In our expedition into East-Central Africa, we will attempt to explore deeply into the geographic heart of the region . . . and into its soul.

**Nkole Mugabe (King), c. 1905** *The Nkole live in southwestern Uganda between lakes Edward and George and the Tanzania border. The Nkole were traditionally divided into two distinct groups, the pastoral Hima and the agricultural Iru, the overwhelming majority. The Hima live in scattered huts, subsisting almost entirely on the product of their herd—but the tall, fair-skinned people managed to dominate the Iru. The Nkole maintained a despotic state headed by the* mugabe, *who received an oath of fealty from the Hima chiefs—and the various Hima chiefs collected tribute from the Iru. The Nkole numbered about 1.5 million in the late twentieth century. This photograph was taken by A.F.R. Wollaston, a noted British naturalist and explorer. In 1914 the Royal Geographical Society awarded Wollaston the Gill Memorial Award "for his exploring work in Central Africa."*

# An Untamed Land

All parts of Africa inspire visitors and students on a grand scale. Some features are the same from region to region. Others are radically different, from the desert north to the rocky Cape of Good Hope at the lower tip. Jungles, mountains, grassy plains, the rich river valleys of the Niger, Congo, and Nile. . . . each area has nurtured an unique collection of animal and plant life. Each has drawn certain combinations of human races and ethnic groups, with their varied customs, religions, and languages.

The east-central realm of the continent varies in appearance, climate, and natural resources. The Indian Ocean in the east washes bright, white, sandy beaches and coral; great mountains and lakes beckon to the west. Fascinating plants abound: olive, *acacia,* coconut, and pungent-scented eucalyptus trees, to name but a few.

Elephants, wild boars, leopards, impalas, giraffes, hippos, crocodiles, and many other awesome creatures—"zoo animals," in the minds of Americans—roam the land and waterside. Exotic birds look down from treetops. Two of the world's most poisonous snakes, the mamba and cobra, lurk in swamplands and savannas, where grass in some places grows taller than humans. Mountain gorillas make their home in Rwanda's northern mountains. (It was from this region that shocking news emerged in

**East Africa Coast and the Peopling of Kenya's Interior, Thirteenth to Nineteenth Centuries.**

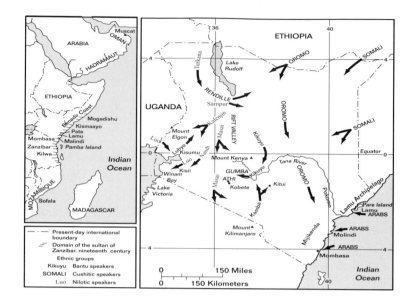

1985: Dian Fossey, an American scientist living among the endangered gorillas and trying to protect them, apparently was murdered by poachers.)

Lake Victoria—second-largest freshwater lake on earth and largest in Africa—is bordered by Kenya, Uganda, and Tanzania. Another important body of water is Lake Tanganyika, the world's second-deepest lake. It separates Tanzania from the Democratic Republic of the Congo, lying in a north-south finger between Burundi to the north and Zambia. The beauty of Lake Tanganyika lures tourists from around the globe.

The Great Rift Valley is a large geological *fault* extending generally north-south through the western part of East-Central Africa. A valley of alluring scenery, the broad region has revealed to *archaeologists* some of the earliest known human fossils.

East-Central Africa is a land of majestic mountains. Africa's highest peak, famous Mount Kilimanjaro, rises more than 19,000 feet on the border between Tanzania and Kenya. In Rwanda near Lake Kivu are the lofty Virunga volcanic mountains, where Fossey worked and died.

The *equator* passes east-west through the center of the region. Unlike other places around the earth where the equator

**Bwamba, c. 1905** *A.F.R. Wollaston photographed this tribe of people on the lower slopes of the Ruwenzori mountain range in western Uganda. They were living in the Bwamba Pass near the town of Fort Portal.*

means a witheringly hot climate, much of East-Central Africa is relatively cool because of its many mountains.

It is a region of many peoples (more than a hundred native tribes inhabit Tanzania alone). Some of the earth's tallest people live in East-Central Africa, as do some of the smallest. The latter include the Batwa Pygmies, known for their skill with poisoned darts. Journalist Jay Marston in 1937 reported from the Uganda lake country: "The people of the forests and the immensely fertile lava plain range from semi-pygmies to seven-foot giants, and from red-brown and light copper to almost black."

**Konjo, c. 1905**  *A.F.R. Wollaston photographed these Konjo people who live in the hills on the Ugandan side of the Ruwenzori range. They subsist mainly as cultivators of beans, sweet potatoes, and corn. The Ruwenzori mountains were long thought to be the source of the Nile River. Today the mountains are economically important for Uganda because of the copper and cobalt deposits, both mined at Kilembe.*

For our study of East-Central Africa, we will examine six modern-day countries and their pasts: Uganda, Rwanda, and Burundi in the interior (the "lake country"); Tanzania, Kenya, and Somalia on the Indian Ocean coast.

## THE EARLY COAST: AZANIA

Ancient Egyptians and Greek and Roman invaders along Africa's northern and eastern coasts left written records of life thousands of years ago. By contrast, the peoples of East Africa kept no written records. To learn of their past, we rely on oral histories, on the observations of outsiders recorded since the 1800s, and on the scientific detective work of archaeologists and *anthropologists*.

**Turkana Chief, 1906** *The Turkana live in the arid, sandy area of northwestern Kenya from Lake Rudolf (Turkana) to the Ugandan border. They successfully resisted British occupation until 1942.*

*In 1972 a team led by Dr. Richard Leakey found the skull KNM-ER 732 along the eastern shore of Lake Turkana—a major paleontological discovery contributing to the complex attempt to understand human evolution.*

Based on fossil findings by anthropologist L.S.B. Leakey 40 years ago, scientists think primitive humans may have lived in northern Tanzania and southern Kenya for almost 2 million years. They have evidence that inhabitants of the Kenya hills farmed and tended livestock as early as 3,000 years ago. These may have been tribes who came to the area from what is today Ethiopia to the north—part of Africa's historical migration patterns.

We have more details about the East African coast. Ancient Mediterranean-based traders wrote of "Azania"—what is today coastal Kenya, lower Somalia, and upper Tanzania—as early as the first century. Already, natives were trading ivory, tortoise shells (used for making combs), coconut oil, and other African wares with foreign merchants, particularly Arabs. These foreigners were bringing in cloth, iron weapons and tools, wine,

**Turkana Chief, 1923** *The Turkana apparently moved to their present lands in northwestern Kenya about 200 years ago from northeastern Uganda. The Turkana are a pastoral people who diligently care for their cattle, which provide dairy products as well as hides, horn, and bone used in everyday life.*

**Turkana Children, 1923**

and other trade goods. The people of Azania, described as tall and dark-skinned, were both farmers and skilled coastal fishers.

By the eighth century, merchants and fishers from Arabia and India were skirting down the African coast of the Indian Ocean regularly, trading and building settlements. They married natives of the region, which the Arabs called the "Land of Zenj." They learned to speak native languages and came to be accepted by local chiefs. The Arabs established trading centers at Mombasa and many other East African locales, and on some of the coastal islands. In time, some of them became rulers, called *sultans,* of city-states along the coast. The sultans and Arab ruling class lived in fine, stone houses and palaces and dressed in the finest garments brought from trading ports far and wide.

The Arabs' main quests in Africa: ivory and gold. They also took away animal skins and human slaves. In exchange, they traded beads, metals, and cloth. An Arab traveler named

**Sultan of Zanzibar, c. 1921–1927** *Zanzibar's history has been shaped by its proximity to the African continent—it is only 22 miles away. Almost all of the Bantu population are Muslims. The rapid expansion of the slave trade in the late eighteenth and early nineteenth centuries, caused by the demand for plantation labor in North and South America, made Zanzibar central to the slave trade routes into the interior of Africa. In 1890 Great Britain proclaimed a protectorate over the sultanate. Seven years later slavery was abolished—although it continued illegally for at least another generation. With British approval, Khalifa ibn Harub became sultan of Zanzibar in 1911. This leading Muslim prince served as a moderating influence during numerous political crises in the East African area for the next five decades. He died in 1960. This photograph shows one of the sultan's many sons and his retinue.*

al-Masudi described what he saw on the East African coast (the land of "Zanj," as he called it) in A.D. 916:

> The land of Zanj produces wild leopard skins. The people wear them as clothes, or export them to Muslim countries. They are the largest leopard skins and the most beautiful for making saddles . . . . There are many wild elephants in this land but no tame ones. The Zanj do not use them for

war or anything else, but only hunt and kill them for their ivory. It is from this country that come tusks weighing fifty pounds and more. . . .

The Zanj eat bananas . . . but their staple food is millet and a plant called kalari which is pulled out of the earth. . . . They also eat honey and meat. They have many islands where the coconut grows . . .

Historians suspect Polynesian mariners also may have visited East Africa during the first several centuries A.D. By the tenth century, natives even may have hosted traders from China.

## Enter the Europeans

At the end of the fifteenth century, Portuguese navigators began sailing around the Cape of Good Hope from the Atlantic. They were the first modern Europeans to establish themselves in East-Central Africa. Vasco da Gama is believed to have been the first European to see what today is Tanzania, arriving in 1498.

The Portuguese forcibly took control of major trading centers like Mombasa. For the most part, they did not cooperate with the native chiefs and island sultans, but instead seized power and ruled with a heavy hand. They demanded that the old leaders acknowledge the dominion of Portugal and pay heavy taxes in gold and goods. If the sultans refused, the Portuguese laid siege to their cities, capturing and looting them. The Portuguese built a stronghold at Mombasa in 1599 and made it their base of Indian Ocean commerce.

After two centuries, Portugal lost its power to Arab dynasties along the East African coast. Trading magnates from Oman on the southern Arabian coast established an island base at Zanzibar and from there controlled commerce to and from East Africa. In 1841 ruler Sayyid Said in Oman relocated his capital to Zanzibar. His followers also established operations on the African mainland. Until the Europeans returned as colonizers in the late 1800s, key cities along the East African coast were under Arab control.

**Masai Woman and Children, 1913** *The Masai are a nomadic people who range along the Great Rift Valley of Kenya and Tanzania. They exist almost entirely on the meat and milk of their herd. In recent years both governments have encouraged the Masai to relocate to permanent settlements.*

## BETWEEN THE LAKES AND THE SEA

Inland from the coastal ports, newcomers discovered spectacular wildlife and landscapes and intriguing native tribes. The famous Masai people began to dominate the interior of what are today southern Kenya and northern Tanzania during the sixteenth and seventeenth centuries. A branch of the Nilotic language group (from the River Nile), they migrated into the area from the north of the continent. Cattle-herding *nomads* and frightful warriors, the Masai captured the livestock of peoples already living in the area and took over the pasturelands. Well-trained, fleet-footed Masai warriors raided for many miles in every direction, from the ocean coast to Lake Victoria.

At the same time, the Masai made friends and established trade with farming tribes in the region. They intermarried with the Kikuyu, one of the groups of Kenya's central highlands. Although at first hostile to the white exploring parties who entered their lands, by 1900 the Masai tolerated the British colonial authorities.

Masai were respected not only for their bravery in warfare but for their mastery over wild beasts. Whites marveled at their method of killing lions, armed only with spears. The invincible, ferocious reputation of the Masai was, of course, somewhat exaggerated. One of their greatest weaknesses was division within; the Masai were not one united people but a group of independent units who sometimes fought against one another. As wandering herders, they also were exposed to natural crises. A cattle disease called *rinderpest,* for example, killed off much of their food supply in the 1890s.

Farther west, near the eastern shore of Lake Victoria, animal life was especially profuse. In what is today the Serengeti National Park, more than a million wildebeest still make their seasonal migrations across the plains as in centuries past. Large herds of gazelles and zebras are among the dozens of other Serengeti animal species and the hundreds of bird varieties.

## Uganda Before the Colonial Era

People of the Bantu tongue are thought to have come to present-day Uganda and Tanzania from Central Africa by 500 B.C. Others moved down from the Nile region of Sudan. Over the centuries, the merging of Bantu and Arab peoples produced the famous Swahili culture.

Three powerful kingdoms arose in what is now Uganda: Buganda, Bunyoro, and Ankole. Meanwhile, other ethnic groups were coming into the area. The Bunyoro people took every advantage of the bountiful lake region. They hunted, farmed, and herded livestock. They also raided neighboring peoples to increase their own wealth. By the 1600s the tribes of Buganda, the banana-growing neighbors of the Bunyoro, on the northwestern

**Roan Antelope, Tanganyika, 1917** *Tanganyika is noted for its wildlife. The Serengeti Plain still supports large migratory herds of zebra, antelope, gnu, rhinoceroses, hippopotamuses, giraffes, gazelles, as well as lions, leopards, cheetahs, and wild dogs. The Serengeti National Park, southeast of Lake Victoria, was established in 1951 and includes within its boundaries some of the best grassland range in Africa.*

coast of what now is Lake Victoria, had responded by banding into a strong, centralized kingdom. The Bugandan king was called the *kabaka.*

Bugandans had no need to provoke their neighbors because their own land was highly productive. The Bugandan farming system proved very lucrative to the kabaka and the local chiefs beneath him. Hordes of peasants raised the crops and paid taxes; they also built roads and performed other labor.

Set well into the African interior, Uganda was not visited by Europeans or Arabs until the 1840s. Muslim traders venturing inland from the coastal ports and southward from Khartoum in Sudan found in the Buganda kingdom two items of great interest: ivory from elephant carcasses and slaves captured by native

**Buganda Village, c. 1920** *During the nineteenth century, Buganda was a powerful kingdom in East Africa in present south-central Uganda. It was one of the several kingdoms founded by the Bantu-speaking peoples. In 1894 Buganda became part of the British sphere of influence, and in 1900 it became a British protectorate. The Ganda people subsequently played an important role in the British administration of East Africa.*

raiders in various parts of the interior. To acquire them, the Muslims exchanged cloth, trinkets, and firearms. This ruthless pattern of trade was common in other regions of the continent, as well.

With the so-called "carving up of Africa" by the European powers in the late 1800s, which we'll examine in the next chapter, Uganda became a British territory along with neighboring Kenya.

## Early Rwanda and Burundi

Directly to the south of Uganda, the native kingdoms of Rwanda and Burundi had been established by the 1700s. Their histories are rooted in ethnic conflict. Twa Pygmies, believed to have been the first humans in the Rwanda/Burundi area, still live in East-Central Africa. Although physically small, they were recognized for their bravery in the wild. About A.D. 1000, the Hutu people moved into the region and soon outnumbered the Twa. Another major group, the Tutsi, arrived during the 1400s and became the rulers of the land.

**Tutsi and Hutu Chiefs, c. 1911** *These Tutsi and Hutu chiefs were photographed in Rwanda-Burundi near Lake Kivu and the Ugandan border. From 1894 to 1918, Rwanda and Burundi were part of German East Africa. German commercial interests began to make inroads in this area in the early 1880s, and German governmental claims to the region were officially recognized by other European powers between 1885 and 1894.*

Through the centuries, Hutus have been the largest population group in Rwanda and Burundi, but Tutsis have held power. Rwanda by the late 1700s was ruled by Tutsi kings, or *mwami*. The Hutus became serfs.

Tension between the Tutsi and Hutu groups thus has existed for hundreds of years. In the 1960s, after Burundi and Rwanda became independent, it exploded into recurring civil strife that continues even now.

African observers find it interesting that the Hutu and Tutsi people, whose clashes in Rwanda and Burundi have been cata-

**Hutu Man, c. 1920** *This Hutu man is wearing a skirt made from banana leaves, a traditional sign of mourning.*

strophic, speak the same language. The peoples look much the same, have notable cultural similarities, and sometimes inter-marry. The main distinction is their way of making a living: Throughout history, Tutsis have been cattle herders, while Hutus have farmed the soil.

The Belgian colonial administration began requiring native blacks to carry ID cards showing whether they were Hutu or Tutsi in 1933.

## ON THE "HORN"

In Somalia, on the "horn" of Africa, Arab traders many centuries ago came across tribes of nomadic livestock herders. In time, Persia gained control of the northern part of the country, along the Gulf of Aden. Zeila, located just below modern-day Djibouti, was a lively Arab port by A.D. 900.

The lower coastal region of the horn of Africa fell under the sway of the island sultans of Zanzibar.

## ZANZIBAR

The main island off the Tanzanian (formerly Tanganyikan) coast is Zanzibar. It was under Arab dominion for centuries before the Portuguese arrived in 1503. Then, for almost 200 years, Portuguese traders operated from the island until Arabs forced them off. In 1861 the island sultan declared independence from mainland Tanganyika.

Until Britain began using its navy, then its army, to thwart African slave trade in the 1800s, Zanzibar flourished—and languished—as an Arab-run slave hub. Raiding parties would hustle through the East-Central African interior, stunning the villages and carrying off ablebodied humans. By the time the captives were brought to the coast, strung together by their necks with ropes, many of them would be stumbling under the burdens of ivory tusks—an additional means of profit to Zanzibar traders. (One ivory tusk was worth approximately $50 to $100, an amount that represented more than a months' wages for many Americans at the turn of the twentieth century.)

Some of the slaves would be kept to serve on the island; others would be shipped to the Persian Gulf. During the late 1700s and early 1800s, slaves taken from East Africa even were shipped around the Cape of Good Hope, across the Atlantic to the Americas. At the peak of the slave trade, slavers were selling an estimated 70,000 East Africans a year.

A British navy lieutenant named L. W. Mathews was with the nineteenth-century English patrol in African waters, on the lookout for illegal slaving vessels. He wrote, "The slaves [in the holds of transport ships] are in a most awful state when we get at them, just stewing together, packed like herrings, and one

**British Artilery, East Africa Protectorate, c. 1907–08**

mass of smallpox, many of them dead, and they and the living cooped up as tight as they can fit in."

When British interference wrecked slave commerce, ivory trade took its place. Ivory—the white tusks of elephants—was carved into beautiful tools and objects of art by African crafters and was used in Europe to make such items as piano keys and knife handles. The "best ivory in the world," one journalist wrote in 1912, came from "Italian Somaliland" to the north. Middlemen up and down East Africa transported tusks to Zanzibar for shipment abroad.

Zanzibar town, on the island's west coast, acquired a reputation as one of the continent's filthiest ports before the colonial era. Arab traders reportedly did not consider it their responsibility to bury slaves who died of torture and tribulation, so they simply dumped the bodies on the beaches for the tides to "bury." In town, bath water and cooking waste were dashed out windows and doors onto the streets.

During the colonial decades, Zanzibar found a humane new source of income: cloves, the aromatic spice used for flavoring

**East Aftrican Expedition Using Porters, 1908.** *Several interpretations can be given to this unusual photograph.*

food. They began to be planted in Zanzibar in the 1860s and were found to flourish. By the early 1900s an estimated 90 percent of the world's cloves were produced in Zanzibar, largely with labor by former slaves who had become tenant farmers.

Zanzibar's strength, though, was not in what it grew but in where it lay. It became one of the southern hemisphere's busiest ports. From the horn of Africa (Somalia) to the southern cape, great quantities of raw materials were transported through the mainland by *porter* and caravan to the coast, and sent across by boat to Zanzibar. The African traders returned home from Zanzibar with loads of foreign-made knives, cloth, and other goods.

## DIFFICULT AND EYE~OPENING EXPEDITIONS TO THE LAKE COUNTRY

In the years before rail transport, trade between Lake Victoria and the Indian Ocean coast was conducted by caravan. During the mid-1800s, Arabs based on the island of Zanzibar opened new caravan paths to Lake Nyasa and beyond, into Central Africa.

White explorers began probing the East African interior about the same time. Johann Krapf and Johann Rebmann's German party in 1847–1849 became the first whites to view spectacular mounts Kenya and Kilimanjaro. (Most people in their home country disbelieved their reports of heavenward, snow-capped peaks so near the equator!) Rebmann wrote the following in his journal on May 11, 1848:

> In the midst of a great wilderness, full of wild beasts, such as rhinoceroses, buffaloes, and elephants, we slept beneath thorn-bushes, quietly and securely under God's gracious protection! This morning we discerned the mountains of Jagga more distinctly than ever; and about ten o'clock, I fancied I saw the summit of one of them covered with a dazzling white cloud. My guide called the white which I saw, merely *Beredi,* cold; it was perfectly clear to me, however, that it could be nothing else but snow. . . .

Richard Francis Burton and John Hanning Speke, British explorers attempting to identify the River Nile's source, reached Lake Tanganyika overland from the Indian Ocean coast in 1858. Speke, in a solo foray northward, saw the southern edge of Lake Victoria. In time, it would be proved that Lake Victoria feeds the Nile; Lake Tanganyika does not. A few years later, Speke traveled from the lake country down the Nile all the way to the Mediterranean Sea. He is believed to have been the first white man to visit what today is Uganda.

In his journal in July/August 1858, Speke provided a glimpse of the East African interior as the whites found it:

> The quantity of cattle in Msalala surpasses anything I have seen in Africa. Large droves, tended by a few men each, are to be seen in every direction over the extensive plains, and every village is filled with them at night. The cultivation also is as abundant as the cattle are numerous, and the climate is delightful. To walk till breakfast, 9 a.m., every morning, I find a luxury, and from that time till

**Mkamba, Tanganyika, 1928** *Except for the narrow coastal belt of the mainland and the offshore islands, most of Tanganyika (now Tanzania) consists of plains and plateaus. Within its boundaries, though, is Africa's highest mountain, Kilimanjaro, and the world's second deepest lake, Tanganyika. This photograph is a village scene from a town in central Tanganyika.*

noon I ride with pleasure; but the next three hours, though pleasant in a hut, are too warm to be agreeable under hard exertion. The evenings and the mornings, again, are particularly serene, and the night, after 10 p.m., so cold as to render a blanket necessary. But then it must be remembered that all the country about these latitudes . . . is at an altitude of from 3500 to 4000 feet. . . .

Eleven days later, he wrote,

To-day's track lay for the first half of the way over a jungly depression, where we saw ostriches, florikans, and the small Saltiana antelopes; but as their shyness did not allow of an open approach, I amused myself by shooting partridges. During the remainder of the way, the caravan threaded between villages and cultivation lying in small valleys, or crossed over low hills, accomplishing a total distance of twelve miles. Here we put up at a village called Ukumbi, occupied by the Walaswanda tribe.

And two days later, on first seeing Lake Victoria and its islands:

This view was one which, even in a well-known and explored country, would have arrested the traveller by its peaceful beauty. The islands, each swelling in a gentle slope to a rounded summit, clothed with wood between the rugged angular closely-cropping rocks of granite, seemed mirrored in the calm surface of the lake; on which I here and there detected a small black speck, the tiny canoe of some Muanza fisherman. On the gently shelving plain below me, blue smoke curled above the trees, which here and there partially concealed villages and hamlets, their brown thatched roofs contrasting with the emerald green of the beautiful milk-bush, the coral branches of which cluster in such profusion round the cottages, and form alleys and hedgerows about the villages as ornamental as any garden shrub in England. . . .

Joseph Thomson, a good-humored Scotsman just twenty-two years old, found himself unenthusiastically cast into the role of expedition leader in June 1878 when his commander Keith Johnston died of a fever in the wilderness. The only whites in the party, Johnston and Thomson were trekking from Dar es Salaam to probe the Tanganyika lake country for England's Royal Geographical Society.

Distressed and feverish himself, but determined to see the mission through after Johnston's death, Thomson resolutely continued to the lakes. "It would not do to let [the native *bearers* and guides] imagine that there was any hesitation about my future movements," he recorded later, "and I stepped from the hut with my purpose distinctly defined. A basket coffin was at once constructed, and a space cleared in the dense forest. On the day following our leader's death we laid him in his last rest-ing-place, where his grave is now green, as his memory will ever be. He lies at the foot of a large tree festooned with grace-ful creepers, under an arbour of dense evergreen bushes. His name and the date of his death are carved on the bark of the tree, and the chief of the village has undertaken to keep the place clear—a contract, I have since heard, he is faithfully car-rying out."

In his book *To the Central African Lakes and Back,* Thomson wrote of how the European pathfinders made their way in unknown environs:

> As we had now arrived at the confines of the well culti-vated and populous districts, it was necessary to be cau-tious in our movements, not pushing too hastily forward, but taking as our motto "be sure of every step before mak-ing it." As our guide was not certain about the best route for such a large caravan, so as to get food, we decided to send him forward a few marches to report upon the coun-try. In the interval we enjoyed ourselves after various fash-ions . . . I wandered about hunting for beetles and butterflies, beasts, and crawling things of different kinds.

## LIVINGSTONE AND STANLEY

"Dr. Livingstone, I presume?" is one of the most famous quotes in history. It was the greeting reporter and explorer Henry Morton Stanley offered when he finally tracked down missing Scottish missionary David Livingstone in 1871 at Ujiji, on the shore of Lake Tanganyika. During the next few years, Stanley made history by crossing the middle of the continent from coast to coast, thus opening the door to Central Africa— the Congo—for European commerce. This was quite an achievement for a Welshman who once claimed he hated Africa "most heartily."

American and English newspapers paid Stanley well for his first two African explorations. The *New York Herald* sent him to find Livingstone (and win a sensational scoop) in 1871. The *Herald* and the *London Telegraph* dispatched him to cross the

**The Market, Ujiji, Tanganyika, 1928** *Ujiji, on Lake Tanganyika, became an important trading center as early as the 1850s. It was at Ujiji that Henry Morton Stanley found David Livingstone, the Scottish explorer-missionary, in 1871. Stanley greeted him with the famous words, "Dr. Livingstone, I presume?" In 1872 the Royal Geographical Society chose Verney Lovett Cameron to lead a relief expedition to bring supplies to Livingstone. Soon after leaving Zanzibar, Cameron met Livingstone's servants bearing his body. At Ujiji, Cameron recovered some of Livingstone's papers, which are now in the archives of the Royal Geographical Society.*

continent in 1874–1877. Stanley could afford to lead expeditions of not just a few dozen native guides, hunters, and bearers, but hundreds of armed men to quell any threat from native tribes. He established a reputation of heartlessness toward the Africans, once burning the huts of a tribe who blocked his way and twice hanging servants who angered him.

Stanley, it should be pointed out, was not alone in resorting to this approach. German explorer Karl Peters, too, killed some of the natives and burned their villages; he once launched a bloody surprise attack against a tribe with whom he'd made a

**Storage House, Konde Area, Tanganyika, c. 1897–1900** *This Bantu storage house is in the "Konde Land," the southern part of Tanganyika between the coast and the northern part of Lake Nyasa. Most of this area is in the Ruvuma River basin, which divided the German territory from Mozambique. This photograph was taken by Dr. Friedrich Füllenborn, a German medical doctor and anthropologist who lived in Tanganyika from 1897–1900. He co-authored the definitive account of German East Africa (Deutsch-Ost-Afrika, Berlin, 1906, 9 vols.).*

**Bantu House, Konde Area, Tanganyika, c. 1897–1900** *This Bantu house was in the Ruvuma River basin of southern Tanganyika. Dr. Friedrich Füllenborn divided the Tanzanian Bantus into eight distinct tribes. No one group has been either politically or culturally dominant. However, those tribes which were subject to Christian missionary influence and western education during the colonial period are now disproportionately represented in the current governmental administration.*

peace treaty; he was known to punish thieving native servants by having them shot or hanged; and he ordered a raid against a Masai camp because, he claimed, the Masai had refused to assign a guide to his party. Peters's "discipline" was so brutal that in 1897, after being assigned imperial commissioner in German East Africa, his own colonial administration brought him to trial and temporarily dismissed him from office.

For his last two missions (1879–1880 and 1887–1890), Stanley was backed by Belgian King Leopold II. Stanley offered his services to Belgium out of anger because his own government

**"Fish House," Konde Area, Tanganyika, c. 1897–1900** *Füllenborn described this dwelling as a "fish house"—the natives are holding fishing spears. In front are large fish traps.*

showed little interest in the Congo. On those expeditions, he navigated the great River Congo by steamboat and probed the region called "Equatoria," making important treaties with African chiefs. Afterward, Stanley renewed his allegiance to Britain and eventually was knighted. He died in 1904.

Livingstone, a devout Christian missionary turned explorer, lacked the broad publicity that followed on the heels of Stanley's journalistic adventures. However, Livingstone is remembered as one of the most important white explorers of Africa and a staunch opponent of the native slave trade. He also was one of the hardiest sojourners, enduring many difficulties. "I was sorely knocked up by this march from Nyañgwé back to Ujiji," he wrote in his diary in 1871. "In the latter part of it, I felt as if dying on my feet. Almost every step was in pain, the appetite failed, and a little bit of meat caused violent diarrhea, whilst the mind, sorely depressed, reacted on the body. . . . The road covered with angular fragments of quartz was very sore to my feet, which are crammed into ill-made French shoes . . . The dust of the march caused ophthalmia [a painful eye inflammation], like that which afflicted Speke. . . ."

Livingstone died in 1873 in what today is the nation of Zambia. Natives lovingly embalmed his body and carried it to the coast for shipment to London. Livingstone was buried in Westminster Abbey. (Church officials later refused to let Stanley be buried beside him.)

## Savage Traditions

European explorers like Livingstone and Stanley were appalled at the internal African slave trade. In his journal, Stanley recorded the incredible statement of an Arab trader: "Slaves cost nothing, they only require to be gathered." Horrific as it was, that assessment was literally true. Among ruthless African traders, it if you wanted to barter for a single ivory tusk you could expect to pay the dealer *one sheep* . . . or as many as *12 human slaves* . . . in exchange!

Raising the loudest alarms against slave trading were the missionaries who arrived in East Africa during the mid-1800s. Swiss Protestants began work near Mombasa in the 1840s. During the late 1870s the British Protestant Church Missionary Society began sending members to Uganda. They were joined by Roman Catholic missionaries from France. The missionaries labored amid primitive hardships—and many of the natives they converted soon faced persecution and death at the hands of their own people. In Buganda in the 1880s, Kabaka (King) Mwanga had thirty of his young Christian servants burned alive because they refused to join him in perverse sexual acts.

## Western Eyes Turn Toward Africa

Until the 1860s and 1870s, Africa was a section of the globe many westerners were, in the words of historian Robin Hallett, "quite content to ignore." European governments showed only occasional "official" interest in the Dark Continent. They installed government outposts in strategic coastal areas like the Nile and Niger river deltas, but rarely cared to push far inland. England, France, Portugal, and other western powers already held colonies elsewhere in the world, and they understood how costly and uncertain it was to maintain them from a distance. They saw no need to colonize Africa formally unless they were sure the undertaking would bring them great rewards.

For the most part, the few Europeans in Africa before the late 1800s were traders. Typically, they dealt in human cargo. Only after western governments, pressured by Christian societies, outlawed slave trading did white entrepreneurs focus their efforts on other goods from the African interior.

The sturdy explorers who began probing the interior—men like Mungo Park, John Hanning Speke, and David Livingstone—were sent out not by government departments but by private geographical or missionary societies. The western public was eager to learn more about this mysterious land with its boundless natural beauty, strange natives, and grotesque animal life. Their governments, though, merely shrugged.

That was about to change. The rough-hewn trading posts around the continent's edge had shown that African tribes could make valuable partners. Not only could Europeans bring out Africa's natural resources, they also could sell (or trade) goods made in their home factories. Their industries needed new markets; here was one with huge potential.

At issue, as European leaders looked more closely toward Africa, was the long-accepted practice of free trade versus "protected" trade. Free trade meant commercial enterprises of any European country were free to deal with merchants anywhere in Africa. But suppose one country's trading companies could establish a *monopoly*—a "protected" zone—at the mouth of one of Africa's great rivers. If that country commanded all the trade flowing into and out of the interior through this region, it would have an advantage in world trade competition.

The term "protection" had a double meaning. By negotiating trade agreements with important tribal chiefs, the Europeans vowed to use their military power to "protect" their African friends against native enemies. At the same time, the whites clearly were "protecting" their own national interests.

In the 1870s and 1880s, European governments fixed their attention squarely on Africa. "Protectionism," not free trade, was on their minds.

**Market, Mwanza, Tanganyika, 1923** *Mwanza, a port city on Lake Victoria, thrived as a trading center. Since 1928 Mwanza has had a railroad link to Tabora and then to Dar es Salaam. The Sukuma are the principal Bantu-speaking people who live in the Mwanza region. This photograph was taken by G. W. Grabham, a geologist who lived in Khartoum.*

# 2

# CREATING THE COLONIES

Critics called it the "Lunatic Line", a "railroad from nowhere to nowhere." Nowhere No. 1 was the seaport of Mombasa on Kenya's southern coast. Nowhere No. 2 was the East African lake country, 400 miles into the interior.

By the time England completed its daunting project, criticism had turned to respect. *The Times* in London enthused, "The road had frequently to be cut through dense forests or hewn out of the rock, bridges had to be built over streams subject to the sudden rise and fall of tropical rains, in the lowlands malarial fever . . . had to be reckoned with, and the attacks to which working parties were often exposed in the jungle from wild beasts, disturbed for the first time in their hereditary lairs, added a new and serious danger. . . ."

Using Indian and African labor, the British completed the main part of the railroad to Nairobi from 1896 to 1899. A few years later, the rail line reached the Lake Victoria port of Kisumu and crossed Ripon Falls at Jinja, Uganda, on the north shore of the lake. This point was the beginning of the "Victoria Nile" river and, in a sense, the "source" of the great Nile. Eventually, the railroad continued around the lake to Kampala, Uganda's colonial center of trade. By then, water commerce at Kisumu already had begun to increase trade between the Indian Ocean and the African interior beyond Lake Victoria.

It cost £5 million to complete. According to explorer Henry Morton Stanley, Great Britain built the Uganda Railway for two reasons: (1) to put down slave trading in the interior and (2) "to effect an uninterrupted and speedy communication between the sea and what is called the 'Pearl of Africa.'"

Fear of foreign competition was another reason, hardly disguised. At the time, the Europeans' boundary lines in East Africa were vague. Britain and Germany were racing to lay down rails and make new territorial claims. Between 1896 and 1914 Germany completed two major lines inward from the coast in Tanganyika. One of them reached some 600 miles from the seaport of Dar es Salaam to Kigoma on the shore of Lake Tanganyika. A branch of this line veered north to Mwanza at the lower end of Lake Victoria.

While the Germans thus forged an iron bond across its southern colony from sea to lakes, the Uganda Railway made it possible for Britain to control and develop its own East African interior—although Britain did not permit white settlers in Uganda, which became part of British East Africa in 1902. That year, Stanley marveled in a *National Geographic* article that "it only now requires two and a half days to reach Uganda from the sea, whereas it previously occupied months."

Soon Ugandan natives were growing enormous quantities of cotton and were boating or hauling it to the Lake Victoria rail ports for shipment to the sea. The land was good for cotton growing. The arrangements among peasant farmers, their tribal chiefs, and British trading companies were acceptable to all. For a while, this small group of native Africans thrived on a European system of economics. But, in the end, that system would prove a dreadful failure of an experiment for the continent as a whole.

Former American president Theodore Roosevelt, on a hunting/collecting expedition in East Africa in 1909–1910, couldn't resist riding at the very front of the Uganda Railway train engine. (England's future prime minister Winston Churchill enjoyed the same breezy perch on a separate visit by rail.) Roosevelt chronicled the event as follows:

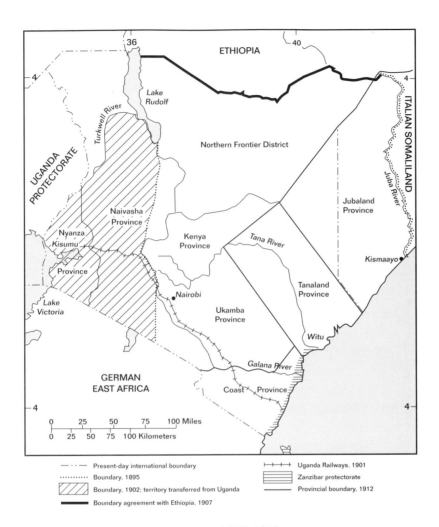

**Kenya—East Africa Protectorate, 1895–1920**

I really doubt if there is a railroad trip in the world as worth taking as that railroad trip up to the little British East African capital of Nairobi. The British government has made a great game preserve of that part of the country. On the trip from the coast, Governor Jackson . . . and the great English hunter Selous and I passed our time on the cowcatcher of the engine, and it was much like going through the Garden of Eden . . . At one spot we would see suddenly six or eight giraffe going off at their peculiar rocking canter. Then we would see a herd of brightly colored hartebeestes, which would pay no attention to the train at all. Then we would come around a curve and the engineer would have to pull his whistle frantically to get the zebras off the track. . . . Then we would see a rhinoceros off to one side; and so on indefinitely.

Railways became vital for travel and transport in East Africa—and remain so today. Around 1910 bicycles were introduced throughout the region. A decade later, the arrival of the first automobiles and trucks meant roads had to be developed and kept in good condition.

## EARLY GERMAN PROBES AND THE GREAT "CARVING UP" CONFERENCE

German expeditions began probing Tanzania and the lake regions of present-day Burundi and Rwanda in the 1880s and 1890s. Soon the area was incorporated into German East Africa. The explorers were joined by Catholic missionaries, who set about to educate and convert native tribes and provide basic medical care.

Most of Germany's claims in Africa were made in a hurried *annexation* scheme from late 1883 to early 1885. An organization called the Society for German Colonization sent representatives to forge treaties with tribal chiefs in what now is Tanzania.

Karl Peters was one of Germany's key explorer-negotiators. Initially sent to East Africa by the Society for German Colonization, he founded his own small colonization society in 1884. The German government discouraged his independent ambitions. In order to dodge German officials, he arrived in Zanzibar from Europe in late 1884 in a mechanic's disguise. Soon, however, he energetically was making treaties for Germany with native chiefs in what would become German East Africa (Tanzania). He survived near-fatal sickness to bring his questionable but ultimately useful treaties out of the interior.

By then, France, England, Portugal, and Spain already had effected realms of control around the coast of the continent. Otto von Bismarck, the powerful German chancellor, believed his country must exert itself in Africa, as well. In fact, Bismarck took the lead. In autumn 1884 he summoned representatives from other European nations to Berlin to discuss a logical, orderly approach to—as he saw it—"helping" Africa. Bismarck and other European leaders decided they should establish a presence on the great continent to improve the lot of the natives and keep peace between the tribes. The Berlin West Africa Conference's General Act, drawn up at the end of the meeting in early 1885, proclaimed that the Europeans must "watch over" African tribes and see to their "moral and material well-being." English poet Rudyard Kipling called this the "White Man's Burden."

Representatives at the conference did not attempt to determine which European countries would control which African territories. They did agree, though, to basic rules for making and honoring their claims. A nation interested in a certain area, they decided, must (1) announce its intentions to other nations and (2) show that it actually exerted authority over the natives in the territory. Until that time, Britain and other countries had claimed African territories based on the mere evidence that their traders and explorers had operated there.

As it happened, German explorer Peters at the time of the conference was negotiating his makeshift treaties with native chiefs in what today is Tanzania—part of the East African realm Britain eyed for itself. Immediately after the Berlin Conference ended, Bismarck staked Germany's claim there, based on Peters's efforts. Suddenly, there was a "German East Africa." The British were alarmed. Diplomats, business leaders, engineers, and others across Europe raced to plan and build rail lines and government stations around the great continent. Each country felt pressure to demonstrate first "authority" over some crucial jungle, desert, or river locale.

From then until the end of the century, European explorers, traders, builders, and soldiers hastened to exert their home countries' control in Africa—sometimes at the risk of international clashes. Historians regard the Berlin Conference as the official beginning of the "scramble for Africa."

## TANGANYIKA AND THE GERMAN HINTERLAND

When the Europeans begun arriving in force during the late 1800s, a powerful king, Kigeri IV, ruled much of present-day Rwanda. Kigeri obtained guns for his army from European coastal traders. Thus equipped, he kept the land basically closed to white intruders.

Interestingly, though, Kigeri allowed his country to be included in German East Africa. Through the German East Africa Company, Germany claimed the territories of "Ruanda" and "Urundi" (modern-day Rwanda and Burundi) as well as much larger Tanganyika (modern-day Tanzania). In 1891, after natives violently rebelled against taxes and enforced labor, the German government took over the holdings of the German East Africa Company. It declared the Tanganyika region a German *protectorate.*

Some of Germany's colonial activities were positive. The colonial government built railroads, as we've seen, and improved farming methods. But native revolts plagued German dominion. During the 1890s, a local ruler named Mkwawa vigorously contested the European presence. Natives staged unnerving surprise attacks on German traders and army patrols. Not until 1899, after Mkwawa committed suicide, did the fighting end.

Peace lasted only a short time. In 1905–1907, southeastern Tanganyika was gripped by the Maji-Maji Rebellion. Natives refused to work the cotton crops as ordered by the German colonial administration. They were tired of the miserable pay and the whippings the overseers administered if workers paused even for a moment to stretch their limbs. Resistance turned to open violence. All foreigners in the area were subject to savage attacks by natives. The rebels—warriors from far-flung tribes with no central leader—came to believe they could repel the Germans' bullets by sprinkling magic water they called *maji-maji* over their bodies.

**Village, Ruvuma River Basin, Tanganyika, c. 1917** *The Ruvuma is the most important river in Tanganyika. It rises in the Matagoro Mountains in southeastern Tanganyika. Flowing eastward, it empties into the Indian Ocean. It is navigable only by small craft for about 60 miles inland. This photograph shows a river village and the overflow of the Ruvuma.*

The water "shield" failed, of course. Soon German reinforcements arrived in the region. Machine-guns mowed down hordes of charging black warriors. Thousands of natives died in the fighting and hundreds of thousands in the famine that occurred at the same period.

German authorities, initially quick to apply force to keep the natives in check, now adopted less harsh policies. They wanted to avert another Maji-Maji Rebellion. Two leaders, colonial minister Bernhard Dernburg and colonial governor Freiherr von Rechenberg, worked to give meaningful support to native farmers and the colony's mission schools. The land was at peace . . . but the Maji-Maji episode showed tribes in German

East Africa that effective resistance to the foreigners might be possible if they joined forces.

Great Britain established a protectorate on the island of Zanzibar in 1890, while Germany controlled mainland Tanganyika. Zanzibar is part of Tanzania today, but for centuries it has existed in many ways independent of mainland East Africa, with a strong Arabian influence.

## NEW PIECES OF THE BRITISH EMPIRE

Britain established its presence in Kenya and Uganda largely by building the long railway through the interior, as discussed previously, and by military force when necessary. Initially British interests in the region were pursued by a commercial organization, the Imperial British East Africa Company. Chartered by the British government in 1888, the company obtained trading rights from the powerful Arab sultan on the island of Zanzibar who controlled the coastal area. Captain Frederick Lugard, an army officer who later became famous for opening much of the Niger basin to British trading interests, led an expedition into Kenya and Uganda in 1890–1892.

The British East Africa Company failed. Seven years after it was established, the company was overwhelmed with financial problems. As the German government had done with the German East Africa Company a few years earlier, the British government took over the company's operations. Britain created its East Africa Protectorate in 1895. Throughout most of the colonial period, the region of modern-day Kenya and Uganda would be known as British East Africa.

Critics of European colonization pointed to the failure of the trading companies as a sign of underlying problems. The white business interests never should have set up operations, they argued, in a distant land where their home governments would be forced to send military protection. It was very costly to maintain armed forces in Africa. Britain had to rely on thousands of native troops in its African army campaigns, led by only a few British officers.

European settlers began arriving in Kenya early in the 1900s. Asians joined them. These foreigners became very influential

**Ugandans, Kampala c. 1920** *Kampala is the capital and the largest city in Uganda. It is located in the southern part of the country just north of Lake Victoria. In 1890 Captain Frederick (later Lord) Lugard chose this site as the headquarters of the Imperial British East Africa Company, one of the chartered companies that preceded imperial annexation. Lugard's fort on Old Kampala Hill remained the Ugandan colonial administrative headquarters until 1905.*

in colonial policies—and some would remain after Kenya became independent in 1963. Whites were not as interested in establishing farm operations in Uganda, so distant from the coast. Thousands of traders from India, Pakistan, and other outside areas developed profitable business ventures there, however. And a bold few farmers from those countries and Europe did move into modern-day Uganda, notably into the kingdom of Buganda.

**Girl Grinding Corn, Kenya, 1913** *The forbidding terrain lying beyond the coast, had given Kenya the reputation among Europeans of being a barren land. During the 1890s, this impression rapidly changed. British soldiers and missionaries reported on the temperate climate and apparent emptiness of the highland region. The area seemed ideal for European settlement and agricultural development using European methods. Very rapidly, traditional native ways of life, their customs and rituals, were changed by European technology.*

Sometimes claiming land where native tribes once had roamed freely, the immigrants developed large farming operations in the Kenyan hill country. If natives wanted to remain on the land, they were expected to serve the newcomers as ill-paid laborers. These colonial white farmers began shipping great volumes of cotton, coffee, and other major crops out of Kenya. Small Ugandan

**Picking Coffee Beans, Kenya, 1908** *The soil and climate of the East African Highlands of Kenya are suitable for coffee growing. Beans labeled "Nairobi" or "Kenya" always have commanded prices at or very near the top of the London market scale.*

*In the 1890s, Kenyan coffee prices stood at record highs. However, ten years later, because of overproduction, prices fell to record lows. And by 1920 the market had virtually collapsed. Yet, in the latter part of the twentieth century, coffee had become one of Kenya's principal export crops.*

farms operated by natives or by Indian and Pakistani settlers added to the growing exports from British East Africa.

By and large, the Indian settlers had less say in colonial affairs than the English farmers. Meanwhile, the natives lived much as they had for centuries: herding, hunting, and growing crops for themselves. Some natives grew additional *cash crops* like cotton or coffee for selling or trading, and a few found meager jobs in cities like Nairobi.

Many native chiefs cooperated closely with the British administrators and missionaries and learned to speak English well. Some held the white administrators in awe. Roosevelt was surprised that some of the literate chiefs he met maintained regular correspondence with him afterward. One sent him a sympathy letter on hearing of the death of Britain's King Edward.

Journalist Jay Marston in 1937 noted the Anglican Cathedral at Namirembe in Uganda: "[O]n a hill opposite stands the mission and cathedral of Rubaga, built by the White Fathers and their lay brethren and converts. One chief gave three forests to provide timber for its beautifully carved woodwork."

In Uganda, the British at first formed an alliance with Mwanga, king of Buganda—then had to fight him in guerrilla warfare. Mwanga had befriended, then persecuted Christian missionaries during the 1880s; he had a similar pro-con relationship with Muslims. He ultimately antagonized the British by accepting a treaty with Germany.

After Britain and Germany signed an agreement in 1890 that gave Britain control of Uganda and Kenya, and Germany control of Tanganyika (Tanzania), the British at first tried to manipulate Mwanga as a puppet native ruler. When he proved uncooperative, they drove him from power.

The British also had to put down resistance from Swahilis in the Kenyan lowlands. Other area chiefs, however, agreed to British-crafted treaties. The whites gave these native tribes token representation in the colonial government, but they claimed large areas of land for Britain and imposed taxes on the natives who lived there. Black chiefs continued to serve as judges over matters concerning their own people but weren't allowed to resolve legal matters in which whites were concerned directly. In short, friendly tribal chiefs provided a useful buffer between the white colonial leaders and the black laboring class.

It was to the whites' advantage to encourage separation among the African tribes. A sense that each group was different from all others kept the natives at odds, to a degree. This, the

**Market at Kibali, c. 1920** *The Kibali Forest is in the region of Lake Tanganyika and Lake Kivu. Note that the boy is wearing bark cloth. Traditionally worn in parts of Uganda, bark cloth is made from the inner bark of certain trees, which is soaked and beaten to reduce the thickness. It is usually dyed and often painted.*

**Ugandan Ruler, c. 1907–1918**

Europeans knew, would make it difficult for the Africans to unify against foreign rule.

Uganda as a colony, with its seat of government at Entebbe, was very different in nature from neighboring Kenya. Dominated by European planters—some of them British *aristocrats*—Kenya came to be considered a "white man's" territory. Uganda, although under British control, was decidedly a "black" land.

## WORLD WAR I: SHAKE-UP AMONG THE EUROPEAN POWERS

We mostly think of gruesome trench warfare in Europe when we think of World War I. Almost unremembered is the African theater. When England, France, and Belgium went to war against Germany, they did so in their homelands as well as their colonies.

In East Africa the colonial governments enlisted or drafted natives to serve in their armies. Throughout the war years, 1914–1918, German East African forces campaigned against those of the British from the north (modern-day Uganda and Kenya) and south (Northern Rhodesia) and those of Belgium from the Congo to the west. Maneuvers in Africa had little effect on the war's outcome, but they had a tragic effect on the native tribes. Soldiers burned villages and devoured crops and cattle on which the Africans depended. Tens of thousands of East African blacks in service died of sickness and starvation.

With its defeat in World War I, Germany lost its colonial holdings. Belgium took over Ruanda-Urundi in 1916, two years before the war's end; Great Britain occupied Tanganyika. Ruanda-Urundi was designated a United Nations "mandate" territory in 1919 and a United Nations "trust" territory in 1946. A Belgian colonial administration governed this area of Ruanda, Urundi, and Tanganyika as part of the Belgian Congo from World War I until it became three separate nations in the early 1960s: Rwanda, Buganda, and Tanzania.

In Tanganyika (Tanzania) after World War I, English administrators tried to govern indirectly through native chiefs. This

*Akidas* **Disguised as Natives to Make an Arrest, Tanganyika, 1921**
*World War I (1914–1918) ended German territorial rule in Africa.
The British advanced into Tanganyika in 1916. Under the Treaty of
Versailles (1919), and then confirmed by the League of Nations,
Great Britain received a mandate to administer Tanganyika, which it
did from 1920 to 1966.*

*Under German rule (1884–1916), a small European staff—
seventy-nine in 1914—had delegated administrative authority to
some 6,000 natives. The official report to the British Parliament in
July 1921 on the transition from German rule noted that most of the
native administrators (akidas) seemed "quite oblivious of native
ideas and customs. It is desirable to eliminate the akidas as soon as
may be possible, for if efficient (as they appear often to be) they are
dangerous."*

**Somali Huts, c. 1912**

strategy basically failed, since there were no regionally dominant tribes or peoples through whom the British could exert
their own powerful influence.

## WORLD WAR II: THE BATTLE FOR THE "HORN"

Up the eastern coast, on the "horn" of the continent, England, France, and Italy all had national interests. The complexi-
ties of the land divisions became starkly apparent after World
War II, as all of Africa approached the end of colonialism. Sort-
ing it out may sound a little confusing. You should refer to a
general map of the area in order to understand the locales and
how they lie in relation to one another.

Across the Gulf of Aden from Somalia, on the Arabian
peninsula, England established a stronghold at the port of Aden

in 1839. To supply the port, it obtained mutton and other foods in Somalia and shipped them across the gulf. British officials arranged trading agreements with Somali native chiefs during the mid-1880s. England proclaimed a protectorate over certain areas in 1887.

At the head of the gulf, France in 1862 claimed the site of Djibouti, where it mined coal. In 1888 England agreed to a boundary between its holdings and those of France around Djibouti. Farther up, along the lower Red Sea, Italy made claims in what is now Eritrea. Italy created its own protectorate in 1889 and expanded it during the coming years. In fact, Italy took over the point of the horn, extending down the Indian Ocean Coast to the Kenyan border.

Historians believe Italy had two basic reasons for colonizing Africa: (1) to relieve its overpopulation at home by sending Italians to live across the Mediterranean and (2) to prove to the rest of Europe that it, too, was an international power player. Settlers from Italy moved in to build plantations around the river locales. By the late 1930s Italy had created an "Italian East Africa." During the colonial period, both British and Italian protectorates were recognized in Somalia.

World War II (1939–1945) placed the two colonies at odds. Italy sided with Germany in the war and thus became Great Britain's enemy. A prelude to the war actually occurred in East Africa, where Italian forces invaded Ethiopia in 1935. Ethiopia—or Abyssinia, as the Europeans called it—was one of only two independent African countries during the colonial era (the other was Liberia on the west coast).

The Italian military remained in control of Ethiopia five years. It also briefly seized British Somaliland in 1940, the year after full-scale fighting began in Europe. The British retook Somaliland. Then, a combined force of black and white British-led troops from across the continent, joined by Belgian and French allies, ousted the Italians from Ethiopia in 1941. England eventually took control of Italian Somaliland.

Five years after the war ended, in 1950, the United Nations allowed Italy to become trustee of its old Somali territory once more. By that point, however, both England and Italy were entering their last years of colonial administration, and they knew it.

**Archetypal Africa** *A lion is attacking a zebra on the savanna. However, on closer inspection, the pair turn out to be fakes. They are stuffed animals, posed in a tableau that creates a popular image of Africa, rather like an exhibit in a museum. This undated photograph was taken in Kenya by Mrs. Will Gordon.*

# 3

# WIDE~EYED WESTERNERS TAKE STOCK

"Africa" came to mean "adventure" in the minds of many Americans and Europeans during the colonial era. They frowned with disapproval at the scant-clad natives and primitive life-styles. But they looked excitedly beyond the villages to the snake-infested jungles, the herds of swift and monstrous animals in the grasslands, the flocks of colorful birds along ancient lakes and rivers, and the snow-capped mountains that beckoned far in the distance. Anticipating Theodore Roosevelt's forthcoming hunting expedition to British East Africa in a 1909 *National Geographic* article, colonial statesman and explorer Sir Harry Johnston said, "I imagine that President Roosevelt will make his starting point Mombasa and that from Mombasa he will probably travel a certain distance on the Uganda Railroad, and then strike off toward the north and see what he can find there in the way of interesting big game." How readers must have yearned to be among the friends and naturalists who went with the beloved hunter-president in his quest for "interesting big game" across the mysterious, boundless continent.

As it turned out, Roosevelt proceeded all the way inland to lakes Victoria and Albert before turning north to follow the River Nile. When Roosevelt's account of his adventure was published two years later, Africa's image as the land of uncounted wildlife surely blossomed even more. He and the scientists with him brought back for American museums "some 14,000 specimens of mammals, birds, reptiles, fishes, etc." Roosevelt traveled with as many as 450 bearers at a time—natives hired to carry the slain animal hides and bones and the expedition's supplies (including ten tons of salt used to cure the skins). "[W]hen we killed elephants, for instance, we would have to use 20 men to carry each elephant's skull."

Keep in mind that Roosevelt was considered a conservationist in his day. "[W]e did not want to kill anything we could help—anything we did not use . . . ," he stated.

"Africa is a land of surprises at every turn," wrote visitor A.F.R. Wollaston in the early 1900s, "so one is not in the least astonished to find lying alongside of the quay at Port Florence [on Lake Victoria], at the end of the Uganda Railway, a perfect little ocean steamship. The white paint and the glistening brass-work, the electric light, and the Indian cook made me think that this was a P. and O. liner eastward-bound rather than a little steamer on a remote lake which fifty years ago no white man had ever seen."

Roosevelt also was taken by the contrast of twentieth-century western civilization "imposed" on ancient African cultures. The Uganda Railway, he marveled, pierced through an awesome region "where man is just as primitive as our cave-dwelling ancestors were a hundred thousand years ago, and where men are fighting practically the same beasts as those ancestors of ours fought."

## THE STRANGE LAND

Westerners who went to colonial East Africa to live and work had gotten a tantalizing glance at the great Dark Continent through the published accounts of precolonial explorers. Especially fascinating were the journals of bold interior trekkers.

Joseph Thomson's book, *To the Central African Lakes and Back,* for example, published in 1881, told of the difference between traveling during the wet and dry seasons in the lake region:

> The rainy season was over, and from a clear cloudless sky the sun beat down with withering effect. The . . . marshes

were replaced by dry, burnt-up deserts, which were extremely painful to traverse, as the mud, during the rains, had been cut up and wrinkled by the feet of wild game into a surface of the greatest irregularity, which had then got baked and hardened by the sun to the consistency of stone. Over this the men painfully limped with their bare feet. Not a drop of running water was to be got, and we had to be content with the slimy water of pits or small ponds, befouled by rotting vegetation. The dense matted bush and tall jungle-grass with which we have become acquainted in Uzaramo, gave place to open ground covered with scattered acacias. These proved to be a terrible nuisance to the bare feet and legs of the porters. The fallen thorns on the pathways were continually getting into their feet, and laming them in the most painful manner.

Even in dry season, though, Africa was a stirring place:

We found the country bordering the river here covered with deep lagoons and back-waters, where myriads of wading and other aquatic birds found a congenial residence. . . .

On the 20th of June we . . . entered a more undulating piece of ground covered with quartz pebbles. We crossed a delicious crystal stream, flowing between richly clad banks, with a sandy bed, the first clear running water we had seen since leaving England. The . . . whole country seemed to have put on a holiday dress to receive us, after the filthy swamps and marshes of Uzaramo, and the deserts of the Rufiji valley. We passed through rich fields of ripened or ripening grain, with natives busily preparing the virgin soil for a second crop. . . . Passing through a perfect tunnel in a tropical forest with its grateful shade, we stepped into an open space winding in a labyrinthine manner among the trees, and dotted with houses which formed the delightful village of Behobeho.

Behobeho, Thomson described, was surrounded by trees and shrubbery so dense that "not a clear bit of ground is seen, and passage through the forest is rendered impossible. From tree to tree hang creepers of every description; slender leafy kinds, swaying gracefully in the breeze; giant forms thick as a man's thigh, gnarled and twisted, binding the tree-trunks as with bands of iron . . . . Here and there, where a break occurs, the creepers may be perceived hanging snake-like from an over-hanging branch, as if ready to strangle the unwary traveller, or forming light festooned bridges from tree to tree for gambolling monkeys to cross. The hoarse cry of the hornbill, or the bark of baboons, are the only sounds which are heard from the forest, though, when darkness sets in, crickets with their fairy chirp, and the weird warning voice of the owl, or the croak of the frogs, help to break the stillness."

## FASCINATING PEOPLES

Roosevelt remarked on the "wide differences among the tribes." Some were farmers living in "beehive huts" and tilling crops. Others were lighter-skinned peoples who herded live-stock in the grasslands and lived in "queer square huts placed in a ring, making what we would call in the West a big corral—a big ring fence in which their cattle are kept."

The Masai and other tribes of Kenya, Roosevelt observed, kept herds of hump-backed cows, goats, "hairy sheep," and donkeys. "They do not till the soil; they live exclusively on meat, blood, and milk."

The Masai fascinate modern observers because of their steadfast insistence on living the way of their ancestors. Masai women are famous for their colorful necklaces. The first whites in East Africa, though, found the Masai more to be feared than admired. For years, explorers pushing toward Lake Victoria and Central Africa from the east took roundabout routes, avoiding the direct approach from the Indian Ocean coast because it would take them through Masai country. Sir Harry Johnston credited the young Scottish adventurer Thomson as "the real founder of British East Africa" because Thomson was the first to make friends with the Masai and gain permission to journey through their lands.

Europeans were astonished to watch Masai men hunt lions armed only with spears and ox-hide shields. Roosevelt described

**Waboni Chief and Family, 1905**  *The Waboni lived along the Tana River between the Kitaru Falls and Mount Kenya in the central part of Kenya. The Tana is Kenya's longest river, about 400 miles, and it flows into the Indian Ocean. The river is navigable for about 150 miles upstream, often with difficulty.*

*This photograph was taken by Alfred Woodhouse who, with T. W. Barber, were the first Europeans to map the course of the Tana River. A tracing of their large-scale map is in the archives of the Royal Geographical Society.*

how several dozen natives cautiously encircled a lion and closed in. Enraged, the lion charged at one man, who carefully "lobbed" his spear into the beast's left shoulder. Other warriors closed round and pierced the lion with fatal wounds—but not without cost. Two of the Masai, Roosevelt wrote, were mauled badly.

**Galla Chief, 1905** *Alfred Woodhouse photographed this Galla chief (left) and his aide along the western section of the Tana River at the village of Oda Boruruba.*

Thomson described an unusual native village in which he stayed in 1878:

The quadrangular huts of the Wazaramo are represented here by simple circular ones, with low walls, huge conical roofs, and broad overhanging eaves. Few of them are more than eight feet in diameter, and as there are neither chimneys nor windows, the smoke of the fires must escape by

**Twa/Pygmy, c. 1920**  *This photograph was taken in the Ruwenzori Mountain Range bordering Uganda and the Congo. The Ruwenzori are considered to be the "Mountains of the Moon" described by Ptolemy, the second-century geographer. These mountains were long thought to be the source of the Nile. In 1913 Captain E. M. Jack, a member of the East African Anglo-German-Belgian Boundary Commission, described the pygmies in this area as "fierce and savage." "These people live on what animals they can snare or kill, and on the food that they steal from their more peaceful neighbors, whose land they are constantly raiding."*

the low doorway. Among these huts you may observe the natives at their several occupations, attired in scanty loin cloths, and with undressed hair.

The Kamba, another interesting group, were noted for their calabash (a type of gourd) carvings. Journalist Jay Marston in the 1930s described some other peoples of the lake region of Uganda:

The semi-pygmies, or Batwa, are reddish-colored men, with puckered faces and wide round eyes. They are skilled trackers and hunters, intrepid in chasing elephants and the gorillas which live high up in the volcanoes . . .

They wield the fire stick cleverly, are all armed with a bow and arrows, and move their villages from place to place as they hunt. They will sometimes dance, and their dances take the form of mock battles.

The young Watussi braves dance too, wonderfully, leaping up high and coming down with ringing stamps. Their Sultan has a special band of dancers. They can also jump over a bar to heights sometimes exceeding the world's official high jump record.

To these people the mountains are gods, which is not surprising, for the massive bulk of the range dominates the country and the lives of those under its shadow.

In general, whites blushed at their first sight of near-naked natives. Theodore Roosevelt wrote,

Another thing about these natives of East Africa: their clothing was very scanty. In one tribe, the Kavirondo, the men and women literally wore nothing. The curious thing was that those people had extremely good manners. They were very courteous and perfectly at ease. . . .

## WONDROUS WILDLIFE

White hunters and explorers who pushed westward toward Central Africa were as amazed by the wildlife as by the natives and their customs. Roosevelt was astounded that in Nairobi, "the wild beasts come right up to the edge of the town. A friend, Mr. McMillan, lent us the use of his house in town while we were staying there, and a leopard came up to the piazza one night after one of the dogs. On another occasion one of the local officials, a district commissioner, going out to dinner on his bicycle in a dress suit, and naturally unarmed, almost ran over a lion."

When a young white settler set out by bicycle one evening to attend a rehearsal for a community play, Roosevelt recounted, she "was knocked off her bicycle by a stampede of zebras, and was really quite hurt and had to give up the rehearsal."

**Mufumbiro (Virunga) Mountain Village, c. 1911** *Captain E. M. Jack described the natives of these mountain villages as "a race of strongly built hardy mountaineers of Bantu type. Their dress consists of skins, though cloth is becoming more common now, and they arrange their hair in long strings or festoons, ornamented with beads, shells, or cent pieces."*

*"The only serious trouble experienced with natives," wrote Jack, "[occurred] when a chieftainess named Mumusa raised the standard of revolt and announced her intention of driving all Europeans out of the country. Mumusa is a well-known person in this part of Africa . . . She is what is known as a 'witch-doctor,' that is, a person regarded by the natives as semi-divine; and she at one time wielded enormous power. On this occasion she collected a considerable following, who looted everywhere and spread great distress. Captain Reid, who was at the time the acting Political Officer at Kigezi, arranged to attack her, and as many men as could be spared from the Commission escort were sent to cooperate. . . . He surprised Mumusa, and captured her and many of her retainers, and scattered the remainder. She was removed to Entebbe, where she remains in durance more or less vile."*

Young Thomson stared wide-eyed at the great numbers of animals feeding at the foot of Tanganyika's mighty mountains:

There, towards the base of Kilimanjaro, are three great herds of buffalo slowly and leisurely moving up from the lower grazing-grounds to the shelter of the forest for their daily snooze and rumination in its gloomy depths. Further out on the plains, enormous numbers of the harmless but fierce-looking wildebeest continue their grazing, some erratic members of the herd gambolling and galloping about with waving tail and strange, uncouth movements. Mixed with these are to be seen companies of that loveli- est of all large game, the zebra, conspicuous in their beau- tiful striped skin, here marching with stately step, with heads bent down, there enjoying themselves by kicking their heels in mid-air or running open-mouthed to mimic fight, anon standing as if transfixed, with heads erect and projecting ears, watching the caravan pass. But these are not all. Look! Down in that grassy bottom there are sev- eral specimens of the great, unwieldy rhinoceros, with horns stuck on their noses in a most offensive and pugna- cious manner. Over that ridge a troop of ostriches are scudding away out of reach of danger . . . . See how numerous are the herds of hartebeest, and notice the graceful pallah springing into mid-air with great bounds, as if in pure enjoyment of existence. There also, among the tall reeds near the marsh, you perceive the dignified waterbuck, in twos and threes, leisurely cropping the dewy grass. The wart-hog, disturbed at his morning's feast, clears off in a bee-line with tail erect, and with a steady military trot truly comical. These do not exhaust the list, for there are many other species of game . . .

Marston, visiting Uganda in the mid-1930s, described an idyllic excursion to famous Murchison Falls near Lake Albert:

At Mutizba, the little port, there was a flat-bottomed steamer, which at midnight started off northward for Murchison Falls. A full moon, dramatically huge and bril- liant, silvered the calm surface of the water and eclipsed all but the bravest stars. The boat anchored at the mouth of the Victoria Nile to await the dawn. . . .

Antelopes of various kinds grazed here, or posed like natural history museum groups, on sun-warmed slabs of rock. Crocodiles in incredible numbers basked, open-mouthed, on sandy banks by the water's edge, slithering in as the boat drew near them.

Hippos, literally by the hundreds, splashed and dived and yawned cavernously in the shallow bays, their wet, red-brown hides and enormous horse-heads glistening. Troops of monkeys played in the trees. Once our native helmsman . . . pointed to a herd of elephants moving in the bush on the right bank."

Wollaston was captivated by a herd of hippopotami bathing in a small lake in western Uganda:

For a moment nothing is to be seen, then suddenly a score or more of huge heads burst through the surface with loud snorts and squirting jets of water through their nostrils. They stare round with their ugly little piglike eyes, yawn prodi-giously, showing a fearful array of tusks and a cavernous throat, and sink with a satisfied gurgle out of sight, to repeat the performance a minute or two afterwards. Sometimes one stands almost upright in the water, then he rolls over with a sounding splashing, showing a broad expanse of back like a huge porpoise. . . . There is something irresistibly suggestive of humanity about their ungainly gambols; only bathing-machines are wanted to complete the picture.

Not all Wollaston's animal observations were so amusing. Along the Ugandan shore of Lake Albert he encountered native fisher tribes who lived in perpetual fear of beastly danger:

At the southeast corner of the lake are some curious colonies of lake-dwellers, whose huts are built several yards from the shore, with the object, presumably, of escaping the attack of the lions, which are always in atten-dance on large herds of game. At a small village at the extreme south end of the lake our camp was surrounded by

**Baby Elephant, Kenya, c. 1890** *The grasslands and lower tree area of Mount Kenya, in south-central Kenya, is a region where elephants thrive—as do buffalo, black rhinoceros, and leopards. Mount Kenya National Park, established in 1949, covers most of this area. These animals were observed elsewhere in Africa as well.*

a high reed-fence for the same purpose, and only a few days before we arrived there a man, who incautiously went outside the fence after dark, had been carried off and eaten.

Yet, Wollaston recognized the lion's useful role in nature's chain. Lion attacks on humans—not part of the animals' natural diet—were rare, he pointed out. "Like the tigers in some parts of India, their favorite food is the wild pigs and small antelopes which play such havoc among the crops, and their complete extermination would not prove to be by any means an unmixed blessing."

A terrifying episode occurred in 1898 in Kenya. For almost a year, a pair of savage lions petrified Indian workers on the Uganda Railway with repeated attacks on their camps near the

River Tsavo bridge site. Bridge engineer John Henry Patterson, after many unsuccessful attempts and near-fatal encounters, finally killed the lions with high-powered rifles. His book, *The Man-Eaters of Tsavo,* became popular, and the mounted lion carcasses went on display at the Field Museum in Chicago . . . but only after hundreds of laborers had been horribly maimed or dragged from their tents and eaten alive.

## PLAGUES AND FEVERS

Strange diseases were the greatest dread of whites bound for Africa. Theodore Roosevelt, commenting on his 1909–1910 hunting expedition, compared the "mild amount of danger in chasing the wild beasts" to the much greater danger of disease in the "fever-haunted lowland."

Roosevelt and other whites in the African wilds religiously boiled water before drinking it, a practice that baffled the natives. *Quinine,* a medicine prescribed at the time to counteract such maladies as malaria, was considered a travel essential. Historian Thomas Packenham has credited "quinine and the steamboat" with opening the unknown reaches of Africa to white explorers in the late 1800s.

British explorer Verney Lovett Cameron, laid up at Tabora (in modern-day Tanzania) in 1873, wrote to a friend, "[O]ut of forty-five days, I have had one fever of eight days' duration, one of seven days, one of five days, one of four days and am now just getting well from a violent attack of headache lasting for five days."

Among the frightening tropical illnesses was sleeping sickness, an inflammation of the brain. Caused by a virus transmitted by a type of fly, it produced fever and constant drowsiness, and ultimately coma and death. Wollaston wrote in 1909 that around Lake Victoria, "enormous areas of the lake-shore and whole archipelagos, where there was a swarming population only a few years ago, have been rendered absolutely desolate by sleeping sickness. I visited a few islands and a strip of shore not far from Entebbe and walked through large grass-grown villages where scattered bones were the only signs of humanity to be seen. It has been computed that more than 200,000 people have died of the disease in Uganda alone during the last seven years . . . . "

Tellingly, the whites' immediate concern seemed to be as much for the inconvenience brought by the disease as for their personal safety. Only four Europeans in Uganda were known to have contracted sleeping sickness, Wollaston reported. However, he lamented "the increasing difficulty of inducing porters and laborers to remain at Entebbe, where they are afraid of catching the disease."

A less harmful but worrisome affliction was a tick-transmitted virus that resulted in a serious fever. Wollaston described it thus: "An ordinary attack lasts for two or three days, and recurs again after an interval of a week or more; in severe cases the attacks may be continued for months." To whites, the most frightening aspect of this fever, as with certain others, was that it had no known cure. Wollaston concluded that "all that can be done is to take steps to avoid being bitten by the tick."

Joseph Thomson, while staying at the village of Behobeho in 1878, reported regular fits of *ague*—fever and chills—"which came on regularly at four o'clock in the afternoon." His expedition leader Keith Johnston meanwhile lay in a nearby hut dying of an unnamed illness. The sick man, Thomson recorded, "became frequently insensible, and gradually grew worse, until the 28th, when he finished his career."

## A HANDFUL OF FOREIGNERS ALTER A CONTINENT

It's remarkable that the European takeover of the great continent, apart from scattered military forays, was effected by a very few whites. Historians Roland Oliver and J.D. Fage observed: "A dozen overworked men could make up the local representatives of a Chartered Company. A consul and two assistants might well form the government of a protectorate."

European administrators, especially in the early years of the colonial period, were running governments on threadbare shoestrings. Funding and staffing from their home countries were dearly limited. Their mission was simply to claim the territory and establish a "presence." Regulating and policing their new-found native subjects was all but impossible outside the colonial capitals.

The results of the new colonial system, though, soon became dramatic. Explorer Henry Morton Stanley in 1902—only a quarter of a century after his famous explorations across the heart of the continent—reflected on the changes he'd observed in East Africa during the last decades of the nineteenth century:

> In those days Mtesa, of Uganda, impaled his victims and clubbed his women to death upon the slightest provocation; the slingers of the islands stood ready to welcome the wayfarer or the traveler with showers of stones, and along all the shores . . . there was a group here and there, or an army at another place doing all the tricks common to barbarous people, and sighing and thirsting for blood. Those days have passed by. The missionaries have been laboring since 1877 in Uganda, and as the result of their labors can show 90,000 Christian people. Three hundred and twenty churches have been established there, and there are many thousands of children at school. . . . The converts of Uganda are now actually carrying the gospel to the distant lands of the west. Toro has been made acquainted with the gospel. Usongora, which was a wild and devastated country only twelve years ago, now welcomes the white traders; at Kavalli, where I rested some months, the people are beginning to take a strong interest in the white man's religion . . . [T]hough missionaries have often felt depressed, broken-hearted, and dispirited, suffered persecution and been expelled from Uganda; though the native converts have suffered torture and death, still the missionaries have persevered, and in the end they have received their reward. They now know that the terminus of the great railway is built on the very shore of the lake, while one steamer, the *William Mackinnon,* is daily trafficking between Port Florence, on the east, and Entebbe, on the northwest. She is the precursor of a fleet of such steamers.
>
> In 1880, 1881, and 1882 I carried three small steamers on to the Upper Congo; today there are eighty, with a

tonnage of about 10,000 tons. Today there is only one steamer of seventy-five feet in length on Victoria Nyanza; in ten years hence there will very likely be fifty, in twelve years one hundred, in fifty years two hundred, and that is the way civilization will go on spreading out and stirring the dark peoples to activity.

By the late 1930s the western influence in East-Central Africa was entrenched. One chronicler noted the "fine 18-hole golf course" just outside Kampala, Uganda—where hippopotami emerged from the nearby river to graze at night. The golf course "occupies the valley of the Kitante River, once a noisome swamp thickly clothed in elephant grass, reeds, and wild date palms; and all around the town are the huts and the banana, sweet potato, cotton, and mubogo patches of the Raganda."

Travel in Africa progressed from foot and beast of burden to bicycle, automobile, and eventually airplane. Journalist Jay Marston, reporting from Uganda in 1939, compared *bush* travel in the early days with travel in the mid-twentieth century:

When the first missionaries, in response to Henry M. Stanley's famous appeal in the *Daily Telegraph,* came to the shores of [Lake Victoria] some sixty years ago, the journey took all of six months [from England]. They walked up from the coast, with their food and kits borne on the woolly heads of Swahili or Wanyamwezi porters, or on the backs of Isabella-colored pack donkeys.

The crossing of the vast and perilous waters in those days was made in canoes of sewn planks, sketchily equipped with broad-bladed paddles, some gourds for baling, and propitiation [sacrifices] to the gods in the form of a few fluttering rags or plantain leaves at the prow.

Small dhows [sailboats] of the Arab pattern also were used.

These early arrivals in Uganda had faced, in their journey inland, all sorts of perils—drought and torrential rains, fevers, and man-eating lions that prowled by night round their camp, hostile tribes, and lake storms of extraordinary violence.

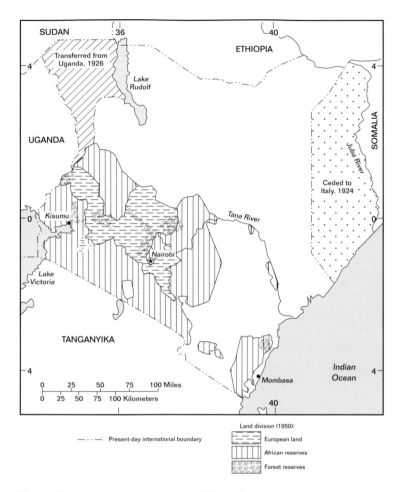

**Kenya Colony and Protectorate, 1920–63**

Nowadays, visitors to Uganda descend from the twice-weekly air liner [to the Entebbe "airdrome"], which has carried them swiftly southward over the spacious desert and swamp and forest of Egypt and the Sudan . . .

They go hither and thither in automobiles, stopping to photograph the beauties of its tropical richness, the wonders of its wild life, its interesting brown peoples, and noticing the marks civilization has made upon it in half a century.

**Native Hut, Kenya, 1906**

# 4

# MOVING TOWARD INDEPENDENCE

Foreign colonials gave native Africans ample reason to crave independence. Soon after they began arriving at the turn of the twentieth century, for example, the British forced many blacks off ancestral lands in order to establish large farms. This included some of Kenya's best terrain, in an area that would become known as the "white highlands." The white settlers took ownership of countless cows, sheep, and goats.

Most foreigners didn't recognize anything wrong in what they were doing. To them, the Africans never were legitimate "landowners" to begin with; they were ignorant heathens who desperately needed outsiders to direct them. As Theodore Roosevelt fondly described them, the natives were "like great big children. They live a perfectly grasshopper life, with no capacity to think of the future."

Explorer Henry Morton Stanley in 1902 publicly commended the missionaries who had labored in the East African interior and the visionaries who had urged construction of the Uganda Railway. "We must also recollect the sagacious administrators who have been sent to Uganda, who, by their tolerance and tact, have taught the natives wherever they go that the advent of the Englishman was a blessing to them."

In hindsight, the negative impact of European colonization on native Africans is obvious. Even at the time, some white visitors already were beginning to realize the problems colonialism brought to Africa. Wollaston wrote in 1909 that "civilization"—that is, western civilization—was largely responsible for spreading the deadly sleeping sickness. "In the old days, when every tribe and almost every village was self-sufficient and had no intercourse with its neighbors, except in the way of warfare, it might very well happen that the disease became localized in a few districts, where its virulence became diminished. Nowadays, with the rapid opening-up of the country, the constant passage of Europeans traveling from one district to another, and the suppression of native warfare, it is becoming increasingly easy for natives to move beyond the limits of their own countries, and by their means sleeping sickness is spread from one end of the country to another."

European administrators quickly found themselves wrestling unsolvable problems. "Governing" any sizeable piece of Africa was fraught with obstacles. It has been hard enough for Africans themselves throughout history (even to the present day). For intruder governments, the complex issues of Africa were bewildering. How could they resolve problems they didn't even understand? The question became simply: Could they maintain peace well enough to extract profits from their African colonies?

The Germans at the turn of the twentieth century and the Belgians who succeeded them took a wise course in running their colonial regimes in Ruanda and Urundi. For the most part, they simply tried to stay on good terms with key Tutsi chiefs. The Tutsi were the real power holders. However, Belgian administrators demonstrated firm overall authority.

European officials left education of the natives in the hands of missionaries. Most whites did not encourage more than a primary school education for Africans. In time, though, a black educated class grew. Its members included teachers, low-level colonial administrators, journalists, merchants, and interpreters. These were the people who would lead the coming groundswell of demands for African independence.

## A Tempest Brews

Native protests sooner or later were unavoidable, in view of the way Europeans had transformed the lives of Africans. In Kenya, as we've seen, tribal peoples watched white planters take over choice lands. The newcomers "allowed" the blacks to stay . . . if the natives were willing to toil for them at ridiculously low wages. Otherwise, the tribes were confined to reserves with less desirable cropland. The British forbade them from growing certain crops in competition with colonial planters and restricted the blacks' travel by requiring them to obtain passes.

Colonial governments forced African men to pay a "head tax" each year. The tax seemed small on paper, but since the natives were paid so abysmally, it was a very heavy burden. They were bound to donate a substantial portion of their own cash crops or commit weeks of labor at white farms and mines—perhaps a great distance from their homes—in order to meet the tax requirement. Did the head tax money go toward improving the lot of the natives? Hardly. It was one way the Europeans financed their own colonial operations.

Across Africa, European commercial enterprises generally manipulated the cash flow—decidedly to the Europeans' advantage. At market, African farmers might be paid less for their crops than colonial planters. In the other direction, European-made goods often were sold to Africans at dramatically hiked prices. Natives had little if any voice in setting prices or making other major decisions. Not for a quarter century was a native African appointed to the legislative council which oversaw the British East Africa protectorate after 1921.

Great Britain had serious trouble in its relations with native Kenyans. As early as the 1920s, blacks began protesting their poor treatment at the hands of British administrators and landowners. The Kikuyu Association, formed in Kenya in 1920, is believed to have been Africa's first political party. In 1922 Harry Thuku, leader of the Young Kikuyu Association, was jailed for leading a rebellion. When his followers in Nairobi tried to free him by force, twenty-one people died.

Between the two world wars, educated Africans founded their own newspapers. Striking a chord with the natives, editors increasingly criticized white colonial policies. Although most Africans were illiterate, the newspapers acquired enormous audiences. Villagers would listen, intrigued, as educated locals read the papers at public gatherings small and large.

A spirit of independence also could be detected among some of the blacks who converted to Christianity. While many natives closely followed the teachings of white missionaries, others formed their own churches and schools. They believed the Gospel message preached by the Europeans, and they took advantage of the basic education the mission schools provided. Yet, they resented certain changes in customs the missionaries urged them to make. Example: In the 1920s the foreigners tried to stop the Kikuyu practice of circumcising young girls. This was a ritual the Kikuyu believed necessary for proper initiation into womanhood.

More and more, Africans resented the colonial system of grossly unfair labor practices, taxes, and military drafts or "encouragement" to fight the white man's wars. Criticism spread. Public acts of protest were erratic, at first. But it became apparent to European leaders that if they were to keep their black subjects under control, they would have to institute meaningful social improvements and grant native representation in colonial administrations. So the colonial governments built new hospitals and schools. They also made at least half-hearted efforts to help the peasant farmers increase cash crop production for the farmers' own benefit.

But by the 1950s those efforts no longer were enough to preserve the colonial system. Too many Africans wanted freedom from the foreigners' yoke.

## DEVELOPMENTS IN BURUNDI AND RWANDA

Remember from our earlier discussion that Burundi and Rwanda are a region of longstanding conflict between the Hutu and Tutsi. The Hutu people began to assert their rights to equality after World War II. They organized political parties, determined to obtain fair participation in government.

Violence erupted between the Hutu and Tutsi in 1959 after a dispute over Rwanda's royal line of succession. It's estimated that as many as 200,000 Tutsi were driven across the borders to neighboring countries—one of the tragic evacuations that would mar the social affairs of Rwanda and Burundi during the late twentieth century. More than 5,000 native huts reportedly were torched.

In 1960 Hutu in Rwanda won popular government elections. They set up a republic in 1961. It was approved by the United Nations, and Belgium acknowledged the country's independence the following year.

At its own independence in 1962 Burundi became a kingdom. (Significantly, the day before independence was proclaimed, the government executed the first of a band of alleged conspirators who had assassinated the provisional prime minister.) In 1966 the nation's first king, Mwami Mwambutsa IV, was ousted by his own son, Ntaré V; within months, Prime Minister Michel Micombero led a military *coup* that overthrew Ntaré. Burundi at that time was made a republic. By that year, 1966, Burundi already had been the scene of ethnic violence between Hutu and Tutsi militants. In 1970 the tension erupted into civil war, taking the lives of more than 100,000 Hutu.

## The Push toward Independence in British East Africa

When the colonial administration of Tanganyika (now Tanzania) in 1951 drove several thousand Meru natives from land white farmers wanted in the north of the country, blacks responded by forming the Tanganyikan African Nationalist Union (TANU). The leader of this political organization was Julius Nyerere, a native educated at universities in Uganda and Scotland.

The TANU grew quickly. Within a few years, it had local organizations in most Tanganyikan villages. Soon it even managed to earn the respect and support of some of the white settlers in the colony. In 1958 the TANU won most of the seats in Tanganyika's elected parliament. Four years later Nyerere would become independent Tanganyika's first president.

Interestingly, Nyerere originally hoped Kenya, Uganda, and Tanganyika would achieve independence not as separate nations, but as a strong *federation.* As those colonies prepared to sever ties with Great Britain in the early 1960s, Nyerere preached that "our strength lies in unity. . . . [T]he boundaries which now divide our countries were made by the imperialists, not by us, and . . . we must not allow them to be used against our unity." Independence proceeded one nation at a time, however. Once each country had tasted self-rule, Nyerere knew, there was little chance their peoples would want to join. As events soon proved, hostility rather than unity among the emerging African nations was more likely.

Meanwhile, in the early to mid-1950s, a militant political force called the Mau Maus (officially, the Freedom Struggle Association) organized a revolt in Kenya. Many of their fighters were Kikuyu, Meru, Emba, and other peoples whose Central Highlands region—excellent farmland—had been taken over by European planters. Mau Mau tactics went beyond passive resistance (strikes) to attacks on the colonial establishment. The rebels first burned white farms and crops and slaughtered cattle, hoping to scare the European settlers into leaving the country. Eventually, they began to attack white colonials—as well as native chiefs who had cooperated with the Europeans.

In 1952 the Mau Mau uprising prompted the Kenyan colonial administration to declare a state of emergency. British troops were hurried to the country (although the government relied on loyal blacks to do much of its fighting during the rebellion). Mau Mau leaders and sympathizers were imprisoned in concentration camps by the thousand. In 1956 a fragile peace was restored.

By the early 1960s it was clear to the British in Kenya and to all the European powers elsewhere that a fully independent Africa was imminent. Tanganyika won independence from Great Britain in late 1961. Kenya was slower to achieve self-government. After gradually gaining a majority of representative seats in the colony's legislative council, Kenya became independent from Great Britain in December 1963, as did the island of Zanzibar.

**Natives Near Embu, c. 1920** *Embu is a town on the Tana River in central Kenya, about 25 miles south of Mount Kenya National Park. It was founded by the British in 1906. In the 1930s, Embu became a Christian missionary center. Today it is a marketing town. Clothing and shoes are manufactured here. The population in 1995 (est.) was 26,000.*

One of the native leaders who had gone to jail for his leadership in the Mau Mau movement, Jomo Kenyatta, became Kenya's first president. Kenyatta had been involved in the Kenyan nationalist movement since the 1920s, when he had been a follower of Thuku. Educated in a Christian mission school, he had studied further in London and had served as a Kenyan government official.

Zanzibar had been rocked by racial violence between the island's black majority and the Arab ruling class. It merged with Tanganyika in April 1964 after islanders revolted against their government in a bloody revolution—more than 10,000 Arabs reportedly were slain or driven off Zanzibar. The resulting United Republic of Tanganyika and Zanzibar quickly took a new name: Tanzania.

In Uganda to the west, internal affairs were complicated by the existence of Buganda, a kingdom within a colony. Locally ruled by King Mutesa II, Buganda was Uganda's richest province. After World War II, the people of Buganda pressed for an independent state. British colonial administrators naturally opposed the idea but were baffled in trying to settle the issue. In 1953, they deported Mutesa because of his opposition to colonial policies. Two years later, they offered Mutesa the nominal title of "king of Uganda"—which angered Ugandans in other areas. Despite regional differences, Mutesa was elected president of Uganda when it became a nation in October 1962. His reign would be fairly short-lived, as we shall see.

## SOMALIA'S STRUGGLE

One of the glaring problems with the colonial system in Africa, critics point out, was that the Europeans "carved up" the continent with little regard for natives' interests, geographical/cultural/religious relationships, or heritage. Some groups of people traditionally hostile toward one another were "assigned" to the same colony, expected to coexist peacefully. Other groups with longstanding ties now were separated by invisible colonial boundaries drawn on paper by politicians and bureaucrats in faraway lands, many of whom had never set foot in Africa.

Later, when the colonies won independence, they didn't go back to the way things were before the 1880s. Instead, they generally built nations defined by the sometimes awkward boundaries the Europeans had drawn for them. In some instances, the national borders arguably were logical. In others, they were literally impossible to maintain in peace.

This kind of boundary dilemma explains much of Somalia's disastrous independence. Italy and Great Britain both gave up control of their "horn of Africa" holdings in 1960. Their two former protectorates, British and Italian Somaliland, became the United Republic of Somalia in July of that year. It was a fragmented land. In the words of British scholar I.M. Lewis several years after independence, "Fighting is common and political solidarity is based upon kinship ties, Somali society as a whole being divided into a vast system of clans and lineages."

Though divided, Somali natives—like others across Africa—yearned for freedom from foreign dominion. During the 1940s the Somali Youth League (SYL) became an influential and popular political party in Italian Somaliland. The SYL organized a preliminary government for Somalia in 1956 and carried general elections in 1959. When the two former protectorates united in 1960, the SYL was central in forming a *coalition* government. It soon faced competition from other parties, however, as well as division within.

From the first, Somalia was plagued by north-south political divisiveness. At the time the former British and Italian territories were joined, there was no practical means of communication between their capitals, Hargeisa in the north and Mogadishu in the south. Within two years, disgruntled army officers in Hargeisa tried unsuccessfully to organize a revolt against the government in Mogadishu, capital of the united republic.

Even more disastrous was feuding over border territories between its neighbors Kenya and Ethiopia. Somalis stubbornly fought for lands they believed were rightfully theirs—lands occupied by peoples of similar ethnic heritage. By 1964 they were engaged in full-scale (though unofficial) warfare on both fronts. And within thirty years, internal and border fighting would plunge Somalia into a state of anarchy.

## STILL TIED BY THREADS OF ASSISTANCE

Independence did not divorce the new African nations entirely from their old European rulers. For example, Belgium supplied vital economic aid to Rwanda and Burundi after giving up its governmental control. Great Britain agreed to multi-million-pound loans to Tanganyika (Tanzania) and in 1964 was asked to help quell a mutiny in the Tanganyikan army. By and large, though, the nations of East-Central Africa now were on their own.

**Giant Ant Spike, 1923**  *This giant ant spike is on the road between Lodwar and Murressi in northeastern Kenya. It is a mound of debris created by ants and termites in digging their nest.*

# 5

# LIFE AFTER INDEPENDENCE

**N**owhere on the continent had native Africans really been prepared to govern themselves democratically. Nor were they prepared to negotiate their way through the late twentieth-century jungle of world politics and markets. Usually the blacks who initially took power in their new nations tried to secure their leadership by force . . . or they soon were deposed by military coups whose leaders secured their own authority by force. In either case, the new African leaders found themselves in charge of a bewildering morass of national and international problems.

Let's look at the progress and trials of East-Central Africa, nation by nation. In the process, we'll examine each country's natural history and features.

## BURUNDI

The Republic of Burundi reflects a classic combination of black African and white European influences. Most of its approximately 6 million people are Hutu (Bantu) descendants. A minority are Tutsi, and about one percent are Twa Pygmies descended from the area's first human residents. White colonialism left prominent marks that continue forty years after independence. Both French and Kirundi are Burundi's official languages today. Swahili, a mixture of native Bantu and outside

**Ugandan Internationally Recognized Administrative Divisions, 1990.**

Arabic tongues, also is a major language. It's notable that almost twice as many people practice Catholicism as native religious beliefs.

Burundi is about as large as the state of Maryland. It is a country of hills and mountains. Lake Tanganyika, which stretches southward from the country's lower boundary, is the world's longest freshwater lake (410 miles) and second-deepest freshwater lake (after Russia's Lake Baikal), reaching 4,710 feet. More than 90 percent of Burundi's inhabitants farm, growing coffee beans and a small volume of cotton and tea. Bujumbura, a city of about 300,000 on Lake Tanganyika, is the capital.

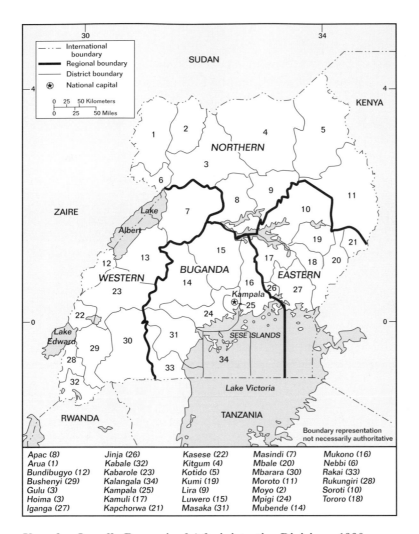

| Apac (8) | Jinja (26) | Kasese (22) | Masindi (7) | Mukono (16) |
| Arua (1) | Kabale (32) | Kitgum (4) | Mbale (20) | Nebbi (6) |
| Bundibugyo (12) | Kabarole (23) | Kotido (5) | Mbarara (30) | Rakai (33) |
| Bushenyi (29) | Kalangala (34) | Kumi (19) | Moroto (11) | Rukungiri (28) |
| Gulu (3) | Kampala (25) | Lira (9) | Moyo (2) | Soroti (10) |
| Hoima (3) | Kamuli (17) | Luwero (15) | Mpigi (24) | Tororo (18) |
| Iganga (27) | Kapchorwa (21) | Masaka (31) | Mubende (14) | |

**Ugandan Locally Recognized Administrative Divisions, 1990.**

The tiny country has had an uncommonly explosive history since independence. Although the Tutsi people constitute only about 14 percent of Burundi's population, they have controlled much of the land, the government, and the army. Tension between the Tutsi and Hutu has been the source of most of Burundi's unrest.

After the civil war of 1970–1971, Burundi's government underwent two military takeovers. Ethnic violence continued periodically. In 1993 free elections were held, and Melchior Ndadaye became the nation's first Hutu president. He was assassinated within months by a Tutsi faction of the military. In the strife that followed, thousands of citizens were killed; many others crossed the borders into neighboring countries for refuge. Shortly after Burundi's parliament appointed Cyprien Ntaryamira president in 1994, the new leader died in the airplane crash we read about at the beginning of our study. Ntaryamira, like Ndadaye, was a Hutu. Enraged at his death, bands of young Hutu militants slaughtered Tutsi citizens. In return, Tutsi soldiers murdered countless Hutu.

In 1996 Major Pierre Buyoya was made president in another military coup. Buyoya, who had been the country's military leader before the 1993 elections, continues in power today.

Violence between Hutu and Tutsi continues. It's estimated that almost a quarter of a million people have been killed in Burundi's ethnic fighting. In 2000 South Africa's internationally famous president Nelson Mandela was named mediator in ongoing negotiations to try to end the bloodshed.

## KENYA

Kenya is one of Africa's most diversely beautiful countries. When western tourists plan a "safari" in Africa, Kenya is a likely destination. It has more than 300 miles of balmy Indian Ocean coastline just below the equator. Dry in its northern zone, it is lush with plant life around Lake Victoria in the southwest. Snow-covered Mount Kenya is Africa's second-highest summit. Vast mountain slopes and valleys provide spectacular backdrops for Kenya's herds of wild beasts. The government has established large wildlife preserves.

Kenya spans 225,000 square miles—about the size of two of America's western states. Just more than 30 million people, most of them farmers, live there. Although most of the labor force works in agriculture, less than 10 percent of Kenya's land is suitable for farming. Small factories produce plastic, wood, and textile products.

The country's people are as different as its geography. Almost fifty ethnic groups are found there. The largest is the

**Kalenjin Warrior, c. 1889** *This photograph is of a Kalenjin warrior of west-central Kenya. During the eighteenth century, Masai expansion pushed the Kalenjin into the area between the Great Rift Valley of East Africa and Lake Victoria where they live today.*

Kikuyu, almost a fourth of Kenya's population, who migrated there about 300 years ago. Luhya, Luo, Kalenjin, and Kamba groups between them account for half the country's people. Historically, the great majority of Kenyans are black Africans.

As a result of European missionary efforts, three-fourths of the people follow either the Protestant or Roman Catholic faiths. Islam has made notable inroads from the north. An estimated 6 percent of Kenyans have clung firmly to the traditional worship forms of their ancestors.

**Kalenjin Chiefs, 1906** *The Kalenjin depend on agriculture for their subsistence. Cattle are also important for providing food but are used, above all, for bride-price payments. Cattle have great ritual importance as well.*

Interestingly, Kenya has both a "national language" (Swahili) and an "official language" (English). A number of other tongues commonly are heard among the different people groups.

During its first decade of independence, Kenya stretched its national wings. It enjoyed a measure of economic growth. Many Europeans and Indians moved away, and Kenya became more African in character. But it also faced difficulties: confrontations among ethnic groups within the country and between Kenya and Somalia, its neighbor to the east. In the 1970s problems mounted. The region was hurt by a drought. New disputes arose between Kenya and two of its other neighbors, Tanzania and Uganda.

Jomo Kenyatta, Kenya's first president, literally went from jail to head of state. He was one of the political activists thrown into prison during the Mau Mau uprising. After becoming president, he caused internal tension by suppressing political rivals. For almost thirty years after independence, Kenya had just one recognized political party: the Kenya African Nationalist Union. Not until 1992, when the nation was rocked by violent political protests, were the first multiparty elections held—and critics charged that they were manipulated by the reigning regime.

Daniel arap Moi has been Kenya's president since 1978, succeeding Kenyatta. The country's economy has languished under his administration. Corruption and discrimination have plagued the government. Fearing a military coup, Moi at one point disbanded the country's air force. He went so far as to order his political opponents arrested if they insulted him.

Moi's policies prompted international outcries. Noted scientist and white Africa native Richard Leakey in 1995 founded a new political party to oppose them. In 1997 the World Bank temporarily refused to issue loans to Kenya.

Natural disasters—floods, major disease epidemics, and drought—contributed to Kenya's woes during the 1990s. Fighting broke out among ethnic groups. In August 1998 the world was shocked when terrorists bombed the United States embassy in Kenya, killing more than 250 people and hurting four times that number.

Apparently in an effort to relieve political pressure from other countries, Moi named his staunch critic Leakey to head Kenya's civil service. The World Bank resumed business with the country.

Nairobi, with a population of more than 2 million, is Kenya's largest city and capital. Mombasa remains its primary seaport.

## RWANDA

Until 1962 the history of Rwanda was largely interwoven with that of Burundi, its neighbor to the south. Even today, the two nations share many of the same kinds of assets and tragic root problems based on ethnic divisions. The two smallest countries in East-Central Africa—and two of the smallest on the whole continent—they have loomed large in the news since independence, with stark headlines following an appalling chain of mass violence.

Slightly smaller than its neighbor Burundi, Rwanda nonetheless has a larger population: more than 7 million. As in Burundi, the great majority of the people belong to the Hutu race. About 19 percent are Tutsi, 1 percent Twa Pygmies. Several languages are prominent in Rwanda: native Kinyarwanda and Swahili and, from colonial days, French and English.

Most of Rwanda's inhabitants are mountain families. More than 90 percent of the people survive by agriculture. Almost two-thirds profess to be Catholics. Others practice animist (native) religions, Protestantism, or Islam.

Rwanda came under Hutu control at its independence in 1962. Grégoire Kayibanda became Rwanda's first president and, twice reelected, served until 1973, when he was ousted in a peaceful military coup. Major General Juvénal Habyarimana, commander of the country's national guard, became head of state. Habyarimana held office twenty years, the last fifteen of them as elected president.

Tutsi-Hutu fighting has plagued the area throughout the years of Rwanda's independence. As we've seen, thousands of Tutsi were driven from the country shortly before independence. Some of them organized an army and tried to recover power in 1963. They failed. Hutu forces retaliated by killing many Tutsi.

From 1990 to 1993, Tutsi exiles living in Uganda renewed a military campaign against the Rwandan government. The clashing forces agreed to form a coalition government in 1993, but after President Habyarimana's plane was downed the following spring, civil war broke out. Some 800,000 Tutsi reportedly were murdered by enraged Hutu, after which Tutsi forces drove almost 2 million Hutu from the country. Altogether, it's believed a fourth of Rwanda's population were either killed or exiled in less than six months.

Many of the refugees fled into the Democratic Republic of the Congo (then called Zaire). Food was short. Disease spread; more than 20,000 people reportedly died of cholera. The misery and death brought about by such a massive influx of homeless people rang an international alarm. In 1996 exiled Rwandans began returning en masse to their country. The homeland was by no means stable, but it offered better hope . . . or less despair . . . than life in the refugee slums.

Some observers believe Hutu were behind the 1994 presidential plane crash. Although Habyarimana himself was a Hutu, he had favored the joint government, angering Hutu militants.

A United Nations court in 1998 tried a former Rwandan government official, Jean Kambanda, for his role in the mass slaughters of 1994. Sentenced to life in prison, he was the first individual from any country convicted under the laws of the international Genocide Convention, passed fifty years earlier.

Paul Kagame, a Tutsi army officer, emerged as the country's military leader in 1994 and became president of Rwanda in April 2000. The former rebel commander, national defense minister, and vice president is the country's first Tutsi president. He has called for peace between the Tutsi and Hutu.

Kigali is Rwanda's capital and largest city.

## Somalia

It's easy to see why the eastern point of the continent is called the "horn of Africa." Resembling the menacing tusk of a rhinoceros, it protrudes some 500 miles into the Indian Ocean, hooking upward to form the lower coast of the Gulf of Aden. Across the water to the north is Saudi Arabia; islands extending from the tip of the horn are Saudi-controlled.

Bending around the shape of the horn is Somalia, a hot, dry land of almost 250,000 square miles (not quite as much territory as the State of Texas) with just more than 7 million people. Somali is the official language. Not surprisingly, because of its

**Somali Warrior, 1912**  *This photograph was taken by I. N. Deacopoli on the Kenyan side of the Somalia-Kenya border. Although European nations drew boundaries, the native peoples usually paid no attention to them.*

*The Royal Geographical Society honored I. N. Deaconpoli in 1914 "for his careful survey and other work in the Sonora desert of Mexico in 1911–1912, and for his East African Expedition of 1912–1913."*

closeness to Arabia, Somalia is an Islamic nation. For a living, most of the people herd, farm, or fish.

Every African nation has faced dramatic difficulties since independence, but perhaps none more than Somalia—one of the continent's poorest countries. Border disputes, civil war, and drought have taken extraordinary tolls. Among the symptoms: Somalia has the highest infant death rate and lowest literacy rate in the region.

Border controversies prompted Somalia to sever diplomatic ties with Great Britain in 1963; Britain released certain challenged territory to Kenya rather than Somalia. Fighting shook both the Kenyan and Ethiopian borders from 1963 to 1967. Part of the dilemma arose from the nature of many border inhabitants—wandering herders whose "citizenship" was hard to define by the standards of colonial boundary lines.

Soon Somalia's internal problems overshadowed outside quarrels. President Abdi Rashid Ali Shermarke was killed in an army coup in 1969. Somalia's legislature was disbanded, state leaders arrested, political parties outlawed. The military regime placed Major General Mohammed Siad Barre in the role of president over the country, which it now called the Somali Democratic Republic.

In 1974 Somalia became part of the Arab League. It also became a Soviet ally. That changed several years later when Russia backed Ethiopia in the continual border dispute between the two African nations. Somalia turned to the United States and Saudi Arabia for support. Fighting between Somali and Ethiopian forces continued for the next decade.

Siad Barre, after failing to take over the eastern areas of Ethiopia, was ousted by rebel factions in 1991. Somalia was given over to guerilla groups. For practically the whole decade of the 1990s Somalia had no effective government. It was a land of fear. Forces in the north seceded and proclaimed a new nation called the Somililand Republic, but did not receive international recognition. In the South, two leaders, Mohammed Ali Mahdi and Mohammed Farah Aydid, both claimed the presidency. Fighting between their followers raged as a drought-caused famine gripped the region. An estimated 300,000 Somalis died.

When the United Nations tried to supervise international relief efforts to the people of Somalia in 1993, they were attacked by the forces of Mohammed Farah Aydid. Americans at home were sickened by news reports showing the bodies of U.S. soldiers being dragged through the streets.

The United States withdrew its forces from the region. By 1995 no U.N. peacekeeping troops remained. Fighting continued among the armed factions in Somalia. (Among the eventual victims: Mohammed Farah Aydid.) Natural calamity—this time widespread flooding—struck again in 1997, adding to the country's miseries.

None of the varying armed factions in Somalia had won control of the country by the turn of the century. At last, in August 2000, a parliament for Somalia was established in the neighboring ministate of Djibouti, and Abdulkassim Salat Hassana was elected president. It remains to be seen whether he will be able to take full control.

There was some positive news during the 1990s: The new Somaliland Republic established a stable government under President Mohammed Ibrahim Egal. Stability also returned to an area on the Gulf of Aden called Puntland, under tribal leadership.

Mogadishu, the ancient Arab trading post on the lower coast of the horn, is Somalia's capital and main port.

## TANZANIA

The southernmost country in the east-central region of Africa, Tanzania is a land of majestic *steppes,* highlands, and lakes. It wraps around the lower half of Lake Victoria in the northwest. Lake Tanganyika forms its border with the Congo to the west, while Lake Malawi (Nyasa) separates it from Malawi in the south. Rising near its northern border with Kenya is renowned Mount Kilimanjaro, highest peak in Africa. About twenty miles off the Tanzanian coast lies the important and unique island of Zanzibar.

Tanzania covers about 365,000 square miles and has a population of some 35 million. Swahili and English are the main languages, Christianity and Muslim the main religions. On the mainland, most people are native Africans, belonging to more

**Ha Women, c. 1921–1923** *Ha, or Waha, are a Bantu-speaking people who live in western Tanzania bordering on Lake Tanganyika. Their area, which comprises grasslands and open woodlands, is called Buha. As in other parts of Africa, agriculture is the primary economic activity. For the Ha, cattle are important as gifts which help establish social ties both at marriage and on other important occasions.*

*The Ha have claimed to live in Buha indefinitely into the past. Arab travelers in the early nineteenth century described them in great detail. They live in dispersed homesteads, normally as an extended family, with a few generations of related males at its core. On a larger scale, Buha existed as six independent kingdoms.*

*The Germans, and later the British, exercised only an indirect control over the Ha. For example, during World War II (1939–1945), the British were unable to force the Ha to work for them. Since Tanzanian independence in 1964, the government has discouraged independent kingdoms and ethnic distinctions. The Ha numbered about 1 million at the end of the twentieth century.*

**Ha Men, c. 1921–1923** *These Ha men are displaying their catch of geese and pigeons.*

than 100 Bantu tribes. On Zanzibar, the Arab influence established by coastal traders more than a thousand years ago remains prominent. As in other East African nations, agriculture is the primary occupation.

When the territory formerly known as Tanganyika became independent in late 1961, it already was influenced heavily by a native political organization called the Tanganyika African National Union (TANU). TANU's leader, Julius Nyerere, became the independent nation's first president in 1962. Two years later Tanganyika merged with the island nation of Zanzibar.

In the late 1970s Tanzania waged a border war with Uganda, as we'll see in our next section. Tanzania essentially won the conflict, driving Ugandan dictator Idi Amin from office. However, the military action hurt Tanzania economically, and Nyerere's government came under international criticism after its occupation of Ugandan territory.

In the aftermath of natural calamities—droughts and floods—Nyerere resigned in 1985. The political leader of the island of Zanzibar, Ali Hassan Mwinyl, took control of the government. He oversaw slow but steady improvements in Tanzania's economy.

When civil war broke out in neighboring Rwanda and Burundi in 1994, hundreds of thousands of people from those countries fled into Tanzania and the Congo. But Tanzania and the Congo were not prepared to meet their needs, and living conditions among the refugees became a matter of international dismay.

Tanzania was cast into an unfavorable light again in 1998, when terrorists bombed the United States embassy in Dar es Salaam. Ten people died. (In the simultaneous embassy bombing in Nairobi, Kenya, as mentioned earlier, some 250 people were killed.)

Benjamin William Mkapa has been president since his election in 1995. He has earned a reputation as a regional peacemaker, seeking to bring warring factions in neighboring lands to the conference table. Mkapa also has worked to improve Tanzania's economy and to reduce forest destruction and pollution. A popular leader, he easily won reelection in 2000—though polling activities were criticized widely.

Dodoma, in the heart of the country, is Tanzania's official capital, but Dar es Salaam—the much larger port city on the Indian Ocean—is where most government offices are located.

## Uganda

Bordered by Sudan on the north and the Congo on the west, Uganda connects East-Central Africa with other major regions of the continent. It's a land of radically different terrain, from desert to swampland. Uganda also is a land of lakes. Lake Victoria is its most prominent waterway. Lakes Albert and Edward lie along the Congo border.

**Village, West Shore of Lake Bunyoni, Uganda, c. 1911** *Captain E. M. Jack, another member of the East African Anglo-German-Belgian Boundary Commission, described Lake Bunyoni in the Mufumbiro [Virunga] mountain range as "a wild and lonely lake in the heart of the mountains. Its sides are so precipitous that nothing is seen of it until one gets quite close. Its waters are deep and cold, and its shores are inhabited by wild and truculent natives." Jack observed a peculiarity of the lake—it contained no fish.*

With a population of about 24 million, mostly farmers, Uganda is one of the most ethnically diverse countries in Africa. The Baganda and Karamojong are the nation's largest ethnic groups—but no group comprises more than 20 percent of the country's population. About two-thirds of Ugandans profess Christianity. Others follow Islam and native religions. English is the official language; several native tongues are common in different parts of the country.

At its independence in 1962, Uganda was considered the richest country in East Africa in terms of natural resources.

**Canoes, Lake Edward, c. 1911** *These canoes drift between the reeds on the Ugandan shore of Lake Edward, one of the major lakes of East Africa.*

Sadly, Uganda's independent government early on was stamped by an almost unprecedented degree of deadly intrigue, persecution, and mass killings.

The king of the area called Buganda, Edward Mutesa, was elected president when the country became a republic. In the years before and after the transition, regional/ethnic issues seriously divided the nation, and Mutesa faced stiff opposition. In 1966 Prime Minister Milton Obote ousted Mutesa from power.

Much of Uganda's dilemma lay in the battle for control between the new national government and the old internal kingdom of Buganda. The British had tried to preserve the

**Lake Bunyoni, 1931** *Lake Bunyoni, in the Mufumbiro (Virunga) mountain range, is on the border of the Congo, Rwanda, and Uganda. There are six volcanoes in the range. The lava flow from the two active ones has reached Lake Kivu in recent years. Today conservationists are attempting to protect the area, both its alpine vegetation as well as its wildlife—which includes the golden monkey and the mountain gorilla.*

Bugandan kingdom. Now, leaders like Obote were determined to dissolve Buganda as a separate entity. Obote's followers won the struggle by force in 1966–1967. Ancient kingships were ended, and the domain of Buganda was carved into four districts.

Opposition to these measures was widespread. Militants tried to assassinate Obote in 1969; he was wounded but survived. Unhappily for Obote, in order to wrest control from Mutesa he had enlisted the help of Colonel Idi Amin of the Ugandan army. In 1971 Amin exiled Obote and seized power for himself.

**Kigezi, c. 1911** *The Kigezi tribe lived on the Ugandan side of the Mufumbiro [Virunga] Mountains. These mountains, north of lake Kivu, extend for almost fifty miles along the border of the Congo, Rwanda, and Uganda. The first major expedition to this area was undertaken by Adolf Friedrich, Duke of Mecklenburg, in 1907–1908. The duke, accompanied by nine other Europeans, brought with him phonograph rolls to record native languages and twelve loads of photographic plates. The Duke wrote a fascinating account of his exploration in Central Africa which was translated into English* (In the Heart of Africa [1910]). *In recent years, the Kigezi Gorilla Game Reserve has been established in this area.*

To say that Amin ruled with an iron hand would be a grotesque understatement. Even on a continent where violent coups, cruel dictatorships, and persecution are all too common, Amin's regime stands out as a "reign of terror." Not content to expel tens of thousands of foreign residents (notably Asians), he began a campaign of death against those he perceived as political enemies and leaders of the church. Amin's forces murdered as many as 300,000 Ugandans, it is believed, often after torturing them. Ugandans lived under strict government

**Mutwali, c. 1911** *This mutwali, or Islamic cleric, was photographed by Major R. E. Critchley-Salmonsen in eastern Uganda. The major worked on the East African Anglo-German-Belgian Boundary Commission in 1911. He donated his many photographs of this region to the Royal Geographical Society.*

control. Opponents repeatedly attempted to oust—or assassinate—Amin, but invariably failed.

Amin made enemies of the United States and Israel. He made friends of militant Arab governments—including those with suspected terrorist ties. In perhaps the most famous skyjacking of the late twentieth century, Palestinian terrorists held passengers hostage aboard a jet at Entebbe, a lake city near the Ugandan capital of Kampala. Israeli commandos stormed the scene and rescued the captives.

An international outcry against Amin brought trade *sanctions*. Uganda's economy, already in serious trouble, suffered further. Most foreign export production ceased. Essentially, Ugandans fished and farmed just enough to feed themselves. Starvation in districts like Karamojong in the north decimated the population. Industrial production plummeted. Rail lines and highways fell into decay.

Amin assumed the title "president for life" in 1976, but his reign was cut short. In the late 1970s, he unsuccessfully tried to seize border areas of neighboring Kenya and Tanzania. Tanzanian President Julius Nyerere previously had been on peaceful terms with Amin. Now Nyerere ordered his army, acting in unison with Ugandan rebels living in exile, to invade Uganda. Amin fled the continent to Saudi Arabia.

After a brief period of failed transitional leaders, Obote was returned to the presidency in 1980 by popular election—although rivals charged voting fraud. Guerilla warfare ravaged the nation, and an estimated 200,000 Ugandans fled to neighboring countries. Obote went into exile after a 1985 army coup. The following year guerilla leader Yoweri Museveni was proclaimed president.

Museveni's reign has been generally positive, although he imposed a ban on political parties for his first decade in office. During his tenure, he has fought government corruption, taken steps to make Uganda more self-reliant, led progress toward better health care (notably, Uganda has reduced its catastrophic AIDS rate), and attracted help from western nations. In the early 1990s Museveni allowed tribal kingships to resume, although the kings have no power in the national government. While Uganda is still plagued by poverty, it is in other respects a dramatically different nation from the Uganda of the 1970s under Amin. Museveni appears to be popular among voters.

**Gisu Chief, c. 1889**  *The Bantu-speaking Gisu live on the western slope of Mount Elgon below the forest zone. Today they cultivate coffee, bananas, and corn. Mount Elgon is an extinct volcano on the Kenya-Uganda border.*

# 6

# A RESTLESS REGION

U nstable" perhaps is the most accurate single word to describe East-Central Africa at the dawn of the twenty-first century. Internal strife has ripped Burundi and Rwanda. Clashes between various countries have contributed to regional unrest during the past 40 years. Idi Amin, president of Uganda in the early 1970s, became hostile toward Rwanda and accused his neighbor of supporting political opposition in his own country. Amin also invaded Tanzania, as we've seen, sparking a war between the two countries.

Outside involvement in internal politics is not uncommon in the region. During the late 1990s Rwandan forces helped political opponents oust Congo leader Mobutu Sese Seko. Rwanda then aided Congolese rebels who opposed Laurent Kabila, the man who replaced Seko. Uganda and Rwanda were so deeply involved in the Congo's power struggle that they joined the signing when a peace accord was reached in 1999 between Kabila and his enemy forces. Soon afterward, fighting broke out among the Congolese rebel factions—shattering the united front Uganda and Rwanda had forged during the complex affair.

To the northeast, Somalia is mired in a longstanding dispute with Ethiopia over control of the Ogaden region. Much of the Somalia-Ethiopia border is a "provisional administrative line." Meanwhile, Tanzania to the south is involved in a boundary controversy with Malawi concerning Lake Malawi (Nyasa), the long waterway that divides the countries.

When internal civil strife spills across national borders, there's sometimes little a neighboring country can do to avoid becoming involved. For example, an estimated 100,000 Hutu died of disease and starvation during Rwanda's civil war of the mid-1990s—not in their native country, but in appallingly crowded refugee camps to which they had fled in the Congo and elsewhere. The Congo simply was unable to accommodate them; even the United Nations was hard-pressed to provide relief.

## REGIONAL ECONOMICS

Coffee, cotton, and tea are important crops throughout most non-desert parts of the region. Livestock is the economic mainstay in Somalia, which also produces large quantities of bananas. Rwanda is noted for its production of an insecticide called pyrethrum, made from flowers. Zanzibar, as we learned earlier, is an island famous for its cloves.

Many of the people farm mostly for their own consumption rather than export. That's hardly surprising, especially in countries like Burundi and Rwanda; ravaged by ethnic civil war, it's been difficult for them to establish an economic foundation beyond *subsistence farming.*

A chronic problem of most East-Central African countries is the fact that they have to import much more than they can export to foreign countries. Africans must rely on foreign aid, some of it from the European countries that once oversaw colonies on the continent.

## HEALTH AND WELFARE

Across Africa, living standards are below those of the industrialized world. Besides the problems caused by ethnic bloodshed, some of the region's urban centers suffer from overcrowding and high poverty levels. Unemployment in Kenya recently was estimated to be as high as 50 percent. The infant death rate in Rwanda and Somalia is reportedly 12 percent or a

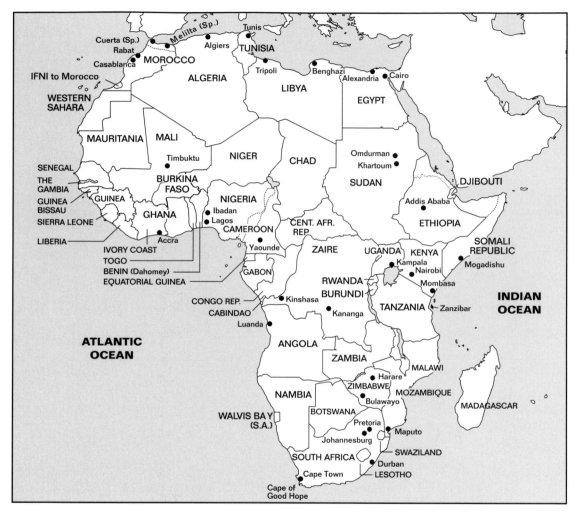

**Modern Day Africa**

little higher. Rwanda has one of the world's worst rates of AIDS. Other nations in the region also have been decimated by AIDS. It's estimated that more than a million citizens of Tanzania, for instance, are HIV-positive.

## Communication and Transportation

Residents of some cities in the region are somewhat "well connected," but in rural areas, modern means of communication are limited. In Burundi, Rwanda, Tanzania, and Uganda,

**Uundwi, Tanganyika, 1928** *Mrs. C. Gordon photographed this family scene during her extensive 1928 expedition through Tanganyika. In 1930, she donated her collection of East African photographs to the Royal Geographical Society.*

you will find one phone line for every 350–450 people. Burundi has one TV set per approximately 240 people, Tanzania one set per 350 people.

Kenya generally is more advanced in communications, with one phone line per 100 people, on the average. It's estimated that 1 in about 10 Kenyans owns a radio, 1 in 40 a television set. In troubled Somalia, little is available in telecommunications.

The Internet is unknown to the overwhelming majority of people in particularly ravaged countries like Rwanda. Kenya and Tanzania, though, each has more than half a dozen Internet service providers; Uganda has three.

No railroads operate in Burundi or Rwanda. They largely depend on the rail systems of neighboring countries for commerce and transportation to/from the coast. Rwanda and

**Hut Building, Kipwa, Tanganyika, 1928** *This photograph, also taken by Mrs. C. Gordon, shows a reed hut in sandy soil. Note the inner construction of the dwelling.*

Burundi are linked to outside rail systems by roads. Somalia, too, is without operative rail lines.

Kenya and Tanzania have the most expansive transport systems. Kenya has about 1,800 miles of railroads, Tanzania about 2,200 miles. Those two countries have about 37,000 and 55,000 miles of roads, respectively. Most roads in the region are unpaved. Rwanda has eight airports or airstrips, Burundi four. Tanzania, by contrast, has about 130, while sprawling Kenya has more than 200.

## Education

The degree of education varies radically among peoples of the region. Recent statistics showed Kenya with a literacy rate

**Native Women, Tanganyika, 1928** *Mrs. Gordon titled this photograph simply "native women." During her 1928 trip through East Africa, Mrs. Gordon spent time with the elusive Sandawe, a Bantu-influenced people living between the Bubu and Mponde rivers. The Sandawe speak a distinctive click language and live in isolated villages.*

of almost 70 percent, one of the highest among the new African nations. Somalia lagged far behind at 24 percent. Literacy in other East-Central African countries ranged from about 40 to 55 percent.

Since independence, some of the governments have made notable efforts to build more schools and universities. Failing economies have hindered progress—as has rampant violence. In Rwanda, for example, public schooling was required for children to age 15, until the civil war of the 1990s caused schools to close.

## CULTURE

As in other regions of the continent, visitors to East-Central Africa are fascinated by native painting and basket, wood, metal, and clay crafts. Complex dance forms and tribal drum

**Chagga Village, c. 1908** *The Kilimanjaro formations in East Africa became known to Europeans in 1848. At first it was not believed that snow-capped mountains existed so close to the equator. Today the Kilimanjaro region is one of Tanzania's leading producers of coffee, barley, wheat, and sugar. This photograph is of a Chagga village on the southern slope of Mount Kilimanjaro in northern Tanzania. The Chagga practice irrigated agriculture on terraced fields, keeping them under constant cultivation through the use of animal manure. Since the 1920s coffee has been their major cash crop. Today, the Chagga are one of the wealthiest of the African peoples.*

**Wakwavi Warriors, c. 1889** *From the 1830s onward, the Great Rift Valley of East Africa was the locale of a succession of internecine conflicts over cattle and grazing grounds. In these wars, the Wakwavi lost their cattle. They were forced to switch to agriculture. The Wakwavi lived between the Great Rift Valley and Lake Victoria.*

music captivated white colonials during the early 1900s and still do today.

The art of storytelling has been refined to a remarkable degree in Tanzania, and it's in this country that some of the world's finest ebony carvings and primitive mask designs derive. The Chagga people of Mount Kilimanjaro are especially noted for their woodwork. In Rwanda, the Tutsi's dramatic ballads recall the traditions of their royal dynasties. Burundi is known for its sophisticated native music and dance.

Western attire has become popular in urban centers. In some more remote areas, meanwhile, people dress much as their forebears did for example, traditional clothing for men in Rwanda is white; Rwandan women wear multicolored clothes.

## SURVIVING IN THE GLOBAL "JUNGLE"

A century ago, journalist Eleanor Stuart jotted down a Zanzibar native's simple summary of life. The man lived in a primitive hut only minutes from his beloved jungle. An African, he told her, is "happier when he lives near to the leopard and the trail of the things that eat and are eaten than when the shadow of a master's hand is always on his shoulder."

East-Central Africans successfully removed the hands of their colonial masters. They still face an ageless problem: the task of living together peacefully. Internal conflicts have a long history and continue still. Now they must find ways to cooperate for common benefits not just with one another, but with distant powers—including the European nations that once overshadowed them. In modern times, the "trail of the things that eat and are eaten" is a trail that encircles the world.

# WORLD WITHOUT END

## DEIRDRE SHIELDS

ONE SUMMER'S DAY in 1830, a group of Englishmen met in London and decided to start a learned society to promote "that most important and entertaining branch of knowledge—Geography," and the Royal Geographical Society (RGS) was born.

The society was formed by the Raleigh Travellers' Club, an exclusive dining club, whose members met over exotic meals to swap tales of their travels. Members included Lord Broughton, who had travelled with the poet Byron, and John Barrow, who had worked in the iron foundries of Liverpool before becoming a force in the British Admiralty.

From the start, the Royal Geographical Society led the world in exploration, acting as patron and inspiration for the great expeditions to Africa, the Poles, and the Northwest Passage, that elusive sea connection between the Atlantic and Pacific. In the scramble to map the world, the society embodied the spirit of the age: that English exploration was a form of benign conquest.

The society's gold medal awards for feats of exploration read like a Who's Who of famous explorers, among them David Livingstone, for his 1855 explorations in Africa; the American explorer Robert Peary, for his 1898 discovery of the "northern termination of the Greenland ice"; Captain Robert Scott, the first Englishman to reach the South Pole, in 1912; and on and on.

Today the society's headquarters, housed in a red-brick Victorian lodge in South Kensington, still has the effect of a gentleman's club, with courteous staff, polished wood floors, and fine paintings.

# AFTERWORD

The building archives the world's most important collection of private exploration papers, maps, documents, and artefacts. Among the RGS's treasures are the hats Livingstone and Henry Morton Stanley wore at their famous meeting ("Dr. Livingstone, I presume?") at Ujiji in 1871, and the chair the dying Livingstone was carried on during his final days in Zambia. The collection also includes models of expedition ships, paintings, dug-out canoes, polar equipment, and Charles Darwin's pocket sextant.

The library's 500,000 images cover the great moments of exploration. Here is Edmund Hillary's shot of Sherpa Tenzing standing on Everest. Here is Captain Lawrence Oates, who deliberately walked out of his tent in a blizzard to his death because his illness threatened to delay Captain Scott's party. Here, too is the American Museum of Natural History's 1920 expedition across the Gobi Desert in dusty convoy (the first to drive motorised vehicles across a desert).

The day I visited, curator Francis Herbert was trying to find maps for five different groups of adventurers at the same time from the largest private map collection in the world. Among the 900,000 items are maps dating to 1482 and ones showing the geology of the moon and thickness of ice in Antarctica, star atlases, and "secret" topographic maps from the former Soviet Union.

The mountaineer John Hunt pitched a type of base camp in a room at the RGS when he organised the 1953 Everest expedition that put Hillary and Tenzing on top of the world. "The society was my base, and source of my encouragement," said the late Lord Hunt, who noted that the nature of that work is different today from what it was when he was the society's president from 1976 to 1980. "When I was involved, there was still a lot of genuine territorial exploration to be done. Now, virtually every important corner—of the land surface, at any rate—has been discovered, and exploration has become more a matter of detail, filling in the big picture."

The RGS has shifted from filling in blanks on maps to providing a lead for the new kind of exploration, under the banner of geography: "I see exploration not so much as a question of 'what' and 'where' anymore, but 'why' and 'how': How does the earth work, the environment function, and how do we manage our resources sustainably?" says the society's director, Dr. Rita Gardner. "Our role today is to answer such questions at the senior level of scientific research," Gardner continues, "through our big, multidisciplinary expeditions, through the smaller expeditions we support and encourage, and by advancing the subject of geography, advising governments, and encouraging wider public understanding. Geography is the subject of the 21st century because it embraces everything—peoples, cultures, landscapes, environments—and pulls them all together."

The society occupies a unique position in world-class exploration. To be invited to speak at the RGS is still regarded as an accolade, the ultimate seal of approval of Swan, who in 1989 became the first person to walk to both the North and South Poles, and who says, "The hairs still stand on the back of my neck when I think about the first time I spoke at the RGS. It was the greatest honour."

The RGS set Swan on the path of his career as an explorer, assisting him with a 1979 expedition retracing Scott's journey to the South Pole. "I was a Mr. Nobody, trying to raise seven million dollars, and getting nowhere," says Swan. "The RGS didn't tell me I was mad—they gave me access to Scott's private papers. From those, I found fifty sponsors who had supported Scott, and persuaded them to fund me. On the basis of a photograph I found of one of his chaps sitting on a box of 'Shell Spirit,' I got Shell to sponsor the fuel for my ship."

The name "Royal Geographical Society" continues to open doors. Although the society's actual membership—some 12,600 "fellows," as they are called—is small, the organisation offers an incomparable network of people, experience, and expertise. This is seen in the work of the Expeditionary Advisory Centre. The EAC was established in 1980 to provide a focus for would-be explorers. If you want to know how to raise sponsorship, handle snakes safely, or find a mechanic for your trip across the Sahara, the EAC can help. Based in Lord Hunt's old Everest office, the EAC funds some 50 small expeditions a year and offers practical training and advice to hundreds more. Its safety tips range from the pragmatic—"In subzero temperatures, metal spectacle frames can cause frostbite (as can earrings and nose-rings)"—to the unnerving—"Remember: A decapitated snake head can still bite."

The EAC is unique, since it is the only centre in the world that helps small-team, low-budget expeditions, thus keeping the amateur—in the best sense of the word—tradition of exploration alive.

# AFTERWORD

"The U.K. still sends out more small expeditions per capita than any other country," says Dr. John Hemming, director of the RGS from 1975 to 1996. During his tenure, Hemming witnessed the growth in exploration-travel. "In the 1960s we'd be dealing with 30 to 40 expeditions a year. By 1997 it was 120, but the quality hadn't gone down—it had gone up. It's a boom time for exploration, and the RGS is right at the heart of it."

While the EAC helps adventure-travellers, it concentrates its funding on scientific field research projects, mostly at the university level. Current projects range from studying the effect of the pet trade on Madagscar's chameleons, to mapping uncharted terrain in the south Ecuadorian cloud forest. Jen Hurst is a typical "graduate" of the EAC. With two fellow Oxford students, she received EAC technical training, support, and a $2,000 grant to do biological surveys in the Kyabobo Range, a new national park in Ghana.

"The RGS's criteria for funding are very strict," says Hurst. "They put you through a real grilling, once you've made your application. They're very tough on safety, and very keen on working alongside people from the host country. The first thing they wanted to be sure of was whether we would involve local students. They're the leaders of good practice in the research field."

When Hurst and her colleagues returned from Ghana in 1994, they presented a case study of their work at an EAC seminar. Their talk prompted a $15,000 award from the BP oil company for them to set up a registered charity, the Kyabobo Conservation Project, to ensure that work in the park continues, and that followup ideas for community-based conservation, social, and education projects are developed. "It's been a great experience, and crucial to the careers we hope to make in environmental work," says Hurst. "And it all started through the RGS."

The RGS is rich in prestige but it is not particularly wealthy in financial terms. Compared to the National Geographic Society in the U.S., the RGS is a pauper. However, bolstered by sponsorship from such companies as British Airways and Discovery Channel Europe, the RGS remains one of Britain's largest organisers of geographical field research overseas.

The ten major projects the society has undertaken over the last 20 or so years have spanned the world, from Pakistan and Oman to Brunei and Australia. The scope is large—hundreds of people are currently working in the field and the emphasis is multidisciplinary, with the aim to break down traditional barriers, not only among the different strands of science but also among nations. This is exploration as The Big Picture, preparing blueprints for governments around the globe to work on. For example, the 1977 Mulu (Sarawak) expedition to Borneo was credited with kick-starting the international concern for tropical rain forests.

The society's three current projects include water and soil erosion studies in Nepal, sustainable land use in Jordan, and a study of the Mascarene Plateau in the western Indian Ocean, to develop ideas on how best to conserve ocean resources in the future.

Projects adhere to a strict code of procedure. "The society works only at the invitation of host governments and in close co-operation with local people," explains Winser. "The findings are published in the host countries first, so they can get the benefit. Ours are long-term projects, looking at processes and trends, adding to the sum of existing knowledge, which is what exploration is about."

Exploration has never been more fashionable in England. More people are travelling adventurously on their own account, and the RGS's increasingly younger membership (the average age has dropped in the last 20 years from over 45 to the early 30s) is exploration-literate and able to make the fine distinctions between adventure / extreme / expedition / scientific travel.

Rebecca Stephens, who in 1993 became the first British woman to summit Everest, says she "pops along on Monday evenings to listen to the lectures." These occasions are sociable, informal affairs, where people find themselves talking to such luminaries as explorer Sir Wilfred Thesiger, who attended Haile Selassie's coronation in Ethiopia in 1930, or David Puttnam, who produced the film *Chariots of Fire* and is a vice president of the RGS. Shortly before his death, Lord Hunt was spotted in deep conversation with the singer George Michael.

Summing up the society's enduring appeal, Shane Winser says, "The Royal Geographical Society is synonymous with exploration, which is seen as something brave and exciting. In a sometimes dull, depressing world, the Royal Geographical Society offers a spirit of adventure people are always attracted to."

# CHRONOLOGY

| | |
|---|---|
| 8th century | Merchants and fishers from Arabia and India are trading and building settlements along the coast of East Africa. |
| Circa 1000 | The Hutu people move into the region of present-day Burundi and Rwanda. Four centuries later the Tutsi arrive and ascend to power. |
| Circa 1500 | Portuguese traders take control of East African ports. Arabs drive them out after two centuries of dominion. |
| 1840s | White explorers begin probing the East African interior. |
| 1884–85 | European leaders discuss their interests in specific African territories at the West African Conference, held in Berlin. Historians consider this the beginning of the "scramble for Africa" by European nations. |
| 1890 | England and Germany agree to an essential division of East-Central African interests. Tanganyika goes to Germany, Kenya and Uganda to England. |
| 1896 | England and Germany begin major rail lines from the Indian Ocean coast to the lake country. |
| 1905–07 | The Maji-Maji rebellion in Tanganyika. |
| 1914–18 | World War I costs Germany its colonial holdings. Ruanda-Urundi comes under Belgian control, Tanganyika under British control. |
| 1920 | The Kikuyu Association in Kenya launches an era of native political activity that will lead to independence. |
| 1939–45 | World War II costs Italy its claims in Somalia—although Italian control is restored over part of the region temporarily in the 1950s. |
| 1952 | The Mau Mau uprising in Kenya. |
| 1961–63 | The former East-Central African colonies become independent. |
| 1970 | Idi Amin's reign of terror begins in Uganda. |
| 1991 | President Mohammed Siad Barre of Somalia is ousted. Somalia becomes a land of anarchy. |
| 1994 | The presidents of Burundi and Rwanda die when their plane is shot down, igniting civil war. |
| 1998 | Terrorists bomb U.S. embassies in Kenya and Tanzania. |
| 2000 | Paul Kagame becomes Rwanda's first Tutsi president. |
| 2000 | South African president Nelson Mandela is named mediator in negotiations between Hutus and Tutsis in East-Central Africa. |
| 2000 | A parliament is established for Somalia in the neighboring ministate of Djibouti; Abdulkassim Salat Hassana is elected president. |

# GLOSSARY

**acacia**—a shrub common to tropical Africa

**ague**—an illness with symptoms of fever, shivering, and sweating

**anarchy**—a society with no system of authority or order

**animism**—a religion that includes the worship of natural objects, including animals and inanimate subjects (rocks, trees)

**annexation**—bringing new territory (usually adjoining land) into an existing government or corporate entity

**anthropologist**—one who studies the origins, behavior, and development of humans

**archaeologist**—one who preserves and studies past human remains

**aristocrat**—a member of a country's upper or ruling class

**bearer**—a native who accompanies an expedition as a supply carrier (same as **porter**)

**bush**—remote, little-populated terrain, often thick with undergrowth

**cash crop**—a crop grown for quick sale locally, rather than for long-term storage/export

**cholera**—an intestinal disease that at times in history has grown into catastrophic epidemics

**coalition**—a usually short-term union of political factions

**consul**—a government's chief representative in a foreign colony

**coup**—a political take-over, which may be violent or peaceful

**equator**—the imaginary east-west circle around the earth at approximately its thickest central part, halfway between the poles

**ethnic**—having to do with the culture, religion, language, race, etc., of a distinct people group

**fault**—a geologic fracture in the earth's crust

**federation**—a union or league of countries

**kabaka**—a king of the Buganda people

**maji-maji**—"magic water" Tanganyikan peasants sprinkled over their bodies to shield them from bullets during their 1905–07 rebellion

**mwami**—ancient kings of the Tutsi people of East Africa

**monopoly**—total control of trade by a single company or nation

**nomad**—a wanderer; a member of a tribe or group who move from one area to another with seasonal changes, herding or hunting

**porter**—see **bearer**

**protectorate**—a country or region under the control and "protection" of a foreign power

**quinine**—a colorless powder or crystalline substance used to treat such diseases as malaria

**republic**—a country ruled not by a king or queen, but by a "popular" government (military factions and dictators have seized power in many African republics)

**rinderpest**—a deadly cattle disease

**sanctions**—in cases such as that of Uganda under Idi Amin, international measures (often economic) to pressure a country to end broad-scale legal violations or inhumane practices

**steppe**—a semi-dry, grassy plains region

**subsistence farming**—growing just enough crops to provide for the needs of a family or tribe

**sultan**—a Muslim ruler

# FURTHER READING

*Africa News* on the World Wide Web at: www.africanews.org

Behrend, Heike. Alice Lakwena and the Holy Spirits: War in Northern Uganda, 1985–97. Athens: Unn. of Ohio Press. 2000.

Foster, Blanche. *East Central Africa.* New York: Franklin Watts. 1981.

Hallett, Robin. *Africa Since 1875: A Modern History.* Ann Arbor, MI: The University of Michigan Press. 1974.

Hanbury-Tenison, Robin, editor. *The Oxford Book of Exploration.* Oxford, England: Oxford University Press. 1993.

Isegawa, Moseg. Apoyssinian Chronicles. New York: Knopf. 2000.

Kanyogonya, Elizabeth, editor, What is Africa's Problem? St. Paul: Unn of Minnesota Press. 2000.

Keay, John, editor. *The Permanent Book of Exploration.* New York: Carroll and Graf, Inc. 1993.

Legum, Colin, editor. *Africa: A Handbook to the Continent.* New York: Frederick A. Praeger, Publishers. 1967.

Oliver, Roland, and J.D. Fage. *A Short History of Africa.* Baltimore: Penguin Books Inc. 1970.

Packenham, Thomas. *The Scramble for Africa: 1876–1912.* New York: Random House. 1991.

Rowell, Trevor. *The Scramble for Africa (c. 1870–1914).* London: B.T. Batsford Ltd. 1986.

Shillington, Kevin. *History of Africa.* New York: St. Martin's Press. 1989.

# INDEX

Abyssinia. *See* Ethiopia
Africa
    approaches end of colonialism,
        65
    archetypal, *68*
    boundary dilemmas in, 94
    coast of East (thirteenth to
        nineteenth centuries), *20*
    European administrators of,
        82–83
    European interest in, 46, 47.
        *See also* Colonialism;
        Colonization
    Europeans encourage separa-
        tion of tribes in, 60, 63
    geography, 19
    "horn" of, 34, 94, 105. *See also*
        Somalia
    independent countries in
        colonial, 66
    modern day, *121*
    westerners ignore, 45–46
Agriculture, 101, 120, 125, 126
    in Burundi, 98
    in Kenya, 100
    in Rwanda, 104
    in Tanzania, 110
    in Uganda, 50, 112
AIDS, 117, 121
Akidas (native administrators)
    (1921), *64*, 64
Albert, Lake, 78, 79, 111
Amin, Idi, 111, 119
    dictatorship of, 114–116
    progress made after, 117
    trade sanctions against, 117
Ankole, 29
Annexation, 52, 57
Anthropologists, 15, 22, 23, 42
Arab League, 107
Arabs
    establish dynasties on East
        Afrian coast, 27
    merging of Bantu and, 29
    quests of, in Africa, 25
    slave trade involvement of, 25,
        45. *See also* Slave trade
    trade of, in Africa, 23, 25, 34
    on Zanzibar, 93–94, 110
Archaeologists, 20, 22
Aydid, Mohammed Farah,
        107–108
Azania, 23, 25

Bantu-speaking peoples, 15, 26,
        42, 97, 110, 118. *See also*
        Hutu
    found kingdom of Buganda,
        31. *See also* Buganda
    Friedrich Füllenborn defines
        tribal divisions of, 43
    merging of Arab and, 29
    in Mwanza region, 48
Barber, T.W., 73
Barre, Mohammed Siad, 107
Batwa. *See also* Batwa Pygmies
    Jay Marston description of,
        75–76
Batwa Pygmies, 21
Bearers. *See* Porters
Belgian Congo, 63. *See also*
        Congo
Belgium
    administration of Territory
        of Ruanda-Urundi by,
        15
    colonial regimes of, 88
    retains ties to Rwanda and
        Burundi, 95
Berlin West Africa Conference
    General Act, 53
    "scramble for Africa," starts at,
        54
    sets down rules for making and
        honoring claims in Africa,
        53
Bismarck, Otto von, 53
British East Africa, 50, 56
    exports from, 58–59
    lack of native representation in,
        89
British East Africa Company, 56,
        57
British Protestant Church
        Missionary Society, 45.
        *See also* Missionaries,
        Christian
Buganda, 29, 60, 113. *See also*
        Uganda
    becomes British protectorate,
        31
    creation of, 63
    dissolution of, 114
    farming system in, 30
    foreign farmers move into,
        57
    kingdom of, 30, 94

king of, 30
    persecution of converted
        natives in, 45
    slaves in, 30–31
    village (c. 1920), *31*
Buha, 109. *See also* Ha
Bunyoni, Lake (Uganda) (1931),
        *114*
    village, west shore of (c. 1911),
        *112*
Bunyoro, 29
Burton, Richard Francis, 37
Burundi, 15, 97–100
    civil war in, 16, 91, 99
    early, 31–33
    farming, 98
    geography, 98
    German expeditions probe,
        52
    independence in, 91
    language, 98
    as part of German East Africa,
        15, 32
    religion, 98
Buyoya, Pierre, 100
Bwamba (c. 1905), *21*

Cameron, Verney Lovett, 41
    describes fevers in Africa,
        81
Caravans, 36–37
Cash crops, 59–60
Chagga
    life of, 125, 126
    village (c. 1908), *125*
Churchill, Winston, 50
Cloves, 35–36, 120. *See also*
        Zanzibar
Coffee, 59, 98, 125
Colonialism, 66. *See also*
        Colonization
    criticism of, 56, 90
    end of, 67
    rules for, set at Berlin West
        Africa Conference, 53
    start of social improvements
        under, 90
Colonization, 56–57, 66. *See also*
        Colonialism
    negative impact of, 88
    problems caused by disregard
        for boundaries created
        under, 94

Congo, 119
  civil war refugees flee to, 111
  disinterest of Great Britain in, 44
  is opened for European
    commerce, 40
  King Leopold II backs Stanley
    expedition of, 43–44
Cotton, 98
  as cash crop, 59–60
  from colonial Kenya, 58
  crops, native refusal to work, 54
Critchley-Salmonsen, R.E., 116

Dark Continent. *See* Africa
Deacopoli, I.N., 106
Democratic Republic of the Congo,
  20, 105. *See also* Congo
Dernburg, Bernhard, 55
*Deutsch-Ost-Afrika* (Füllenborn),
  42
Disease, 29, 39, 81–82, 103, 117,
  121
  effects of colonization on, 88

East Africa, 101
  coast, Arab control of key cities
    along, 27
  competition between Britain and
    Germany for, 53
  daily life in early, 26–27
  early transportation in, 52
  foreign trade of, 25–27
  Ganda people are important to
    British administration of, 31
  hardship of travel in, 70–71
  protectorate (c. 1907–1908),
    British artillery, *35*
  during World War I, 63
East African Anglo-German-
    Belgian Boundary Commis-
    sion, 75, 112, 116
East-Central Africa
  climate, 20–21
  communication and transporta-
    tion, 121–123
  culture, 124, 126–127
  economics, 120
  education, 123–124
  geography, 19–21
  health and welfare, 120–121
  independence comes to most
    nations of, 95
  lakes, 20. *See also* specific lakes

mountains, 20, 21. *See also*
    specific mountains
  peoples of, 21. *See also* Natives;
    specific peoples
  Portuguese establish themselves
    in, 27
  present-day instability of, 119–120
  Twa Pygmies in, 31
  western influence in, by late
    1930s, 84
  wildlife, 19. *See also* Wildlife
Edward, Lake, canoes (c. 1911), *113*
Egal, Mohammed Ibrahim, 108
Elgon, Mount, 118
Emba, 92
Equator, 20–21, 125
Equatoria, 44. *See also* Congo
Ethiopia, 119–120
  invasion of, 66
Ethnic conflict, 15, 31, 32, 99–100,
    103, 120
  between Hutu and Tutsi, 16, 91

Fage, J.D., 82
Fossey, Dian, 20
Fossils, 20, 23
France, 66
Freedom Struggle Association. *See*
    Mau Mau uprising
Free trade, 46, 47
Friedrich, Adolf (Duke of Mecklen-
    burg), 115
Füllenborn, Friedrich, 42, 44
  defines tribal divisions of
    Bantus, 43

Galla chief (1905), *74*
Gama, Vasco da, 27
Ganda, 31. *See also* Buganda
Genocide Convention, 105
German East Africa, 15, 32, 52
  *Deutsch-Ost-Afrika*, as definitive
    account of, 42
  Kigeri IV allows country to be
    included in, 54
German East Africa Company, 54
Germany, 53
  colonial regimes of, 88
  expeditions from, probe areas of
    Africa, 52
  forges treaties in Tanzania, 52
  loss of colonial holdings by, 63
  territorial claims of, 50, 54

Giant ant spike (1923), *96*
Gisu chief (c. 1889), *118*
Gordon, Mrs. C., 122, 123, 124
Gordon, Mrs. Will, 68
Grabham, G.W., 48
Great Britain
  builds Uganda Railway, 49–50
  competes with Germany for East
    Africa, 53
  conflict with Italy during World
    War II, 66
  establishes pretectorate on Zan-
    zibar, 26, 56
  forces natives off ancestral lands,
    87
  retains ties to Tanzania, 95
  thwarts slave trade, 34, 35, 50
  toleration of, by Masai, 29
Great Rift Valley, 20, 101, 126

Habyarimana, Juvénal, 16, 104, 105
Hallett, Robin, 45
Harub, Khalifa ibn, *26*
Hassana, Abdulkassim Salat, 108
Ha (Waha)
  men (c. 1921–1923), *110*
  society of, 109
  women (c. 1921–1923), *109*
Hima, 18. *See also* Nkole
Hutu. *See also* Burundi
  animosity toward Tutsis, 16, 99
  arrival of, 31
  become serfs, 32
  begin to assert rights to equality,
    90
  Belgians require ID cards for, 33
  close connection to Tutsi, of, 15,
    33
  disctinction between Tutsi and,
    33
  efforts to make peace between
    Tutsi and, 105
  as majority, 15, 16, 32, 97, 104
  man (c. 1920), *33*
  and Tutsi chiefs (c. 1911), *32*
  win elections in Rwanda, 91

Internet, 122
*In the Heart of Africa* (Friedrich),
    115
Iru, 18. *See also* Nkole
Islam, 101, 104. *See also* Muslims
Italy, 66–67

Ivory trade, 25
  in Buganda, 30
  connection of slave trade to, 34,
    45
  early, 27
  replaces slave trade, 35

Jack, E.M., 75, 112
  describes trouble with Mumusa,
    77
  description of mountain village
    natives by, 77
Johnston, Harry, 69, 72–73
Johnston, Keith, 39
  death of, 39–40, 82

Kabaka (king), 30. See also
    Buganda
  Mwanga, brutality of, 45
Kabila, Laurent, 119
Kagame, Paul, 105
Kalenjin
  chiefs (1906), 102
  life of, 102
  warrior (c. 1899), 101
Kamba, 75
Kambanda, Jean, 105
Kayibanda, Grégoire, 104
Kenya, 100–103
  baby elephant (c. 1890), 80
  British restrictions in, 89
  climate, 58
  colony and protectorate
    (1920–1963), 85
  East Africa protectorate
    (1895–1920), 51
  ethnic groups in, 100–101
  European technology changes
    native ways of life in, 58
  farming, 101
  geography, 100
  girl grinding corn (1913), 58
  Great Britain establishes pres-
    ence in, 56
  Great Britain gains control of, 60
  immigrants develop large farms
    in, 58
  independence in, 92
  interior, peopling of (thirteenth to
    nineteenth centuries), 20
  internal and external problems
    of, 102–103
  language, 102

mapping of course of Tana River
    in, 73
Masai domination of southern, 28
Mau Maus in, 92. See also Mau
    Mau uprising
Mombasa, 27, 49, 69
native hut (1906), 86
picking coffee beans (1908), 59
political persecution and bomb-
    ings in, 16
religion, 101
settlers arrive in, 56–57
"white highlands" of, 87
as "white man's" territory, 63
Kenya African Nationalist Union,
    103
Kenya, Mount, 73, 100
  first whites view, 37
  wildlife near, 80
Kenyatta, Jomo, 93, 103
Kibali
  Forest, 61
  market at (c. 1920), 61
Kigali, plane crash at, 15, 100, 104
Kigeri IV, 54
Kigezi
  (c. 1911), 115
  Gorilla Game Reserve, 115
Kikuyu, 29, 92, 101
  rites, foreign criticism of, 90
Kikuyu Association, 89
Kilimanjaro, Mount, 20, 108, 125
  description of wildlife near base
    of, 78
  first whites view, 37
  highest mountain in Africa, 38
Kipling, Rudyard, 53
Kitaru Falls, 73
Kivu, Lake, 20, 32, 61, 114
KNM-ER 732, skull, 23. See also
    Leakey, Richard
Konjo
  (c. 1905), 22
  life of, 22
Krapf, Johann, 37

"Land of Zenj," 25. See also East
    Africa
League of Nations, 15, 64
Leakey, L.S.B., 23
Leakey, Richard, 23, 103
Leopold II, King (of Belgium),
    43–44

Lewis, I.M., 95
Livingstone, David
  death of, 41, 45
  description of travel hardships of,
    44–45
  Henry Morton Stanley finds the
    missing, 40
  papers in archives of Royal Geo-
    graphical Society, 41
  sponsors of, 46
  Verney Lovett Cameron brings
    supplies to, 41
Lugard, Frederick, 56
  fort of, 57
"Lunatic Line," 49. See also
    Uganda Railway

Mahdi, Mohammed Ali, 107
Maji-Maji Rebellion, 54–55
  natives learn from, 55–56
Malawi, 120
Malawi (Nyasa), Lake, 108, 120
Mandela, Nelson, 100
Man-Eaters of Tsavo, The (Patter-
    son), 81
Marston, Jay, 21
  compares early travel in Africa to
    mid-twentieth century travel,
    84
  description of Anglican Cathe-
    dral in Uganda, 60
  description of Batwa, 75–76
  description of excursion to
    Murchison Falls, 78–79
Masai, 101
  early explorers fear and avoid, 72
  hunting prowess of, 72–73
  Karl Peters orders raid against,
    43
  life of, 28
  toleration of British colonial
    authorities, 29
  warriors, 28, 29
  woman and children (1913), 28
Matagoro Mountains, 55
Mathews, L.W., description of slave
    trade by, 34–35
Mau Mau uprising, 92–93, 103
Meru, 91, 92
Micombero, Michel, 91
Military coups, 91, 99–100, 103,
    104
Mining, 22, 66

Missionaries, Christian, 43, 44, 52, 83
  are commended by Stanley, 87
  education of natives by, 88, 93
  establish center in Embu, 93
  native chiefs cooperate with, 60
  protest against slave trade, 45, 46
Mkapa, Benjamin William, 111
Mkwawa, 54
Moi, Daniel arap, 103
Monopoly, 46. *See also* "Protected" trade
"Mountains of the Moon," 75. *See also* Ruwenzori mountain range
Mount Kenya National Park, 80, 93
Mtesa, 83
Muanza, 39
Mufumbiro (Virunga) mountain range, 112, 114
  village (c. 1911), *77*
Mumusa, problems with, 77
Murchison Falls, 78–79
Museveni, Yoweri, 117
Muslims, 26, 108, 110, 116. *See also* Arabs; Islam
  trade in early Uganda, 30
Mutesa, Edward, 113
Mutesa II, King, 94. *See also* Mutesa, Edward
Mutwali (c. 1911), *116*
Mwambutsa IV, 91
Mwami (king), 32, 91
Mwanga, 45. *See also* Kabaka
  is driven from power, 60
  pro-con relationship of British and, 60
Mwinyl, Ali Hassan, 111

*National Geographic* magazine, 50, 69
Natives
  colonial mistreatment of, 41, 87, 89
  effects of World War I on, 63
  life of, in British East Africa, 60
  near Embu (c. 1920), *93*
  protests by, 89
  taxes imposed on, 60, 89
Ndadaye, Melchior, 100
Niger River, 46
Nile River, 46
  search for source of, 37
Nilotic language group, 28

Nkole
  life of, 18
  (mugabe) (king) (c. 1905), *18*
Nomads, 28, 34, 107
Ntaré V, 91
Ntaryamira, Cyprien, 15
  death of, 100
Nyasa, Lake, 42
Nyerere, Julius, 91–92, 110
  desires federation, 92
  invades Uganda, 117

Obote, Milton, 113, 114, 117
Oliver, Roland, 82
Oral histories, 22

Packenham, Thomas, 81
Park, Mungo, 46
Patterson, John Henry, 81
Peters, Karl
  brutality of, 41, 43
  colonial administration of, 43
  independent ambitions of, 52
  makes treaties with native chiefs, 52, 53
Poachers, 20
Porters, 70, 84
  (1908), *36*
Portugal, in East-Central Africa, 27, 34
"Protected" trade, 46–47
Protectorate, 26, 35, 51, 56, 66, 85
  Buganda becomes British, 31
  Tanganyika region becomes German, 54
Ptolemy, 75

Quinine, 81

Rebmann, Johann, 37
Rechenberg, Freiherr von, 55
Ripon Falls, 49
Roads, development of, 52
Roosevelt, Theodore
  comments on danger of disease in Africa, 81
  describes differences among natives, 72
  description of Kavirondo, 76
  description of natives, 87
  description of Uganda Railway, 50–52
  description of wildlife near towns, 76

  hunting expedition of, 50, 69–70
  maintains correspondence with native chiefs, 60
  observes Masai hunting lions, 72–73
Royal Geographical Society, 18
  expeditions sponsored by, 39–40
  sends relief expedition to David Livingstone, 41
Ruanda-Urundi, 88. *See also* Burundi; Rwanda; Rwanda-Burundi
  Belgium takes over, 63
  formation of, by League of Nations, 15
Rudolf (Turkana), Lake, 23
Ruvuma river basin, 42, 43
  village (c. 1917), *55*
Ruwenzori mountain range, 21, 22, 75
Rwanda, 104–10?
  civil war in, 16, 91, 104–105, 1?
  creation of, 63
  early, 31–33
  farming, 104
  German expeditions probe, 52
  independence in, 91
  language, 104
  martial law in, 16
  mountain gorillas, 19–20. *See also* Fossey, Dian; Wildlife
  as part of German East Africa, 15, 32
  religion, 104
Rwanda-Burundi, 32. *See also* Burundi; Ruanda-Urundi; Rwanda

Said, Sayyid, 27
Sandawe, 124
Seko, Mobutu Sese, 119
Serengeti National Park, 29, 30
Serengeti Plain, 30
Shermarke, Abdi Rashid Ali, 107
Slavery, abolition of, 26, 46. *See also* Slave trade; Slaves
Slaves, 25, 46
  description of nineteenth-century, 34–35
  former, become tenant farmers, 36
  shipments of, 34

Slave trade, 25
  Arab involvement in, 25, 34, 45
  continuation of illegal, 26
  description of, by L.W. Mathews, 34–35
  in early Uganda, 30–31
  Great Britain tries to stop, 34, 35, 50
  internal African, 45
  Livingstone opposes, 44
  missionaries protest against, 45
  outlawing of, 46
  peak of, 34
  rapid expansion of, 26
  in Zanzibar, 34
Society for German Colonization, 52
Somalia, 119–120
  anarchy in, 95
  Arab traders in, 34
  coalition government in, 95
  difficulties in, 107
  fragmentation of, 94–95
  geography, 105
  huts (c. 1912), 65
  language, 105
  north-south divisiveness of, 95
  politics in, 107
  problems between Kenya and, 102–103
  protectorates in, 66
  religion, 107
  trading agreements between England and, 66
  violence in, 16, 107–108
  warrior from (1912), 106
Somaliland, 66, 94–95. See also Somalia
Somali Youth League (SYL), 95
Speke, John Hanning
  description of East African interior by (1858), 37–39
  sponsors of, 46
  visits Uganda, 37
Stanley, Henry Morton
  commends missionaries, 87
  crosses middle of Africa, 40
  death of, 44
  describes changes in East Africa, 83–84
  heartlessness toward Africans of, 41
  King Leopold II backs Congo expedition of, 43–44

  marvels at Uganda Railway, 50
  New York Herald and London Telegraph sponsor trips of, 40–41
  renews allegiance to Great Britain, 44
  states reasons for building Uganda Railway, 50
  tracks down David Livingstone, 40
Steamers, 83–84
Stuart, Eleanor, 127
  Subsistence farming, 120
Sukuma, 48
Sultans, 26, 27, 34, 56
Swahili, 29, 60, 97, 102, 108

Tana River, 73, 74, 93
Tanganyika. See also Tanzania; Zanzibar
  akidas disguised as natives to make an arrest (1921), 64
  Bantu house, Konde area (c. 1897–1900), 43
  becomes German protectorate, 54
  English governance of, after World War I, 63, 65
  "fish house," Konde area (c. 1897–1900), 44
  geography, 38
  Germany gets control of, 60
  hut building, Kipwa (1928), 123
  independence in, 92
  Maji-Maji Rebellion in, 54–55
  market, Mwanza (1923), 48
  market, Ujiji (1928), 41
  Mkamba (1928), 38
  native women (1928), 124
  roan antelope (1917), 30
  Ruvuma river basin, village, 55
  storage house, Konde area (c. 1897–1900), 42
  Uundwi (1928), 122
  Zanzibar declares independence from, 34
Tanganyika African National Union (TANU), 91, 110
Tanganyika, Lake, 41, 61, 108
  geography, 20
  Royal Geographical Society expedition to, 39–40
  and search for source of Nile River, 37

  Stanley finds Livingstone on shore of, 40
  as tourist attraction, 20
  Tutsi (c. 1921), 14
  world's second deepest lake, 38
Tanzania, 38. See also German East Africa; Tanganyika
  civil war refugees flee to, 111
  creation of, 63
  geography, 108
  German expeditions probe, 52
  language, 108, 110
  Masai domination of northern, 28
  problems between Kenya and, 103
  religion, 108
  Vasco da Gama arrives in, 27
  wars with Uganda, 16, 110–111
Terrorists, 103, 111, 116–117
Thomson, Joseph
  describes ague, 82
  describes making way in unknown environs, 40
  description of interior East Africa trek, 70–71
  description of Kilimanjaro wildlife, 78
  description of Wazaramo village, 74–75
  makes friends with Masai, 72
  Tanganyika lake country expedition of, 39–40
  village of Behobeho, described by, 71–72
Thuku, Harry, 89
To the Central African Lakes and Back (Thomson), 40, 70
Trade agreements
  German, 52
  negotiated with tribal chiefs, 46–47, 52
Trade, early, 23, 25. See also Trade agreements
Transportation, 84
  in East Africa, early, 52
Turkana
  chief (1906), 23
  chief (1923), 24
  children (1923), 25
  life of, 24
  resistance to British occupation of, 23

Tutsi, 88, 91. *See also* Burundi
  animosity toward Hutus, 16, 99
  arrival of, 31
  Belgians require ID cards for, 33
    (c. 1921), *14*
  close connection to Hutu, of, 15,
    33
  disctinction between Hutu and, 33
  efforts to make peace between
    Hutu and, 105
  and Hutu chiefs (c. 1911), *32*
  as minority, 15, 16, 97, 104
  power of, 32
Twa Pygmies, 31, 97, 104
  description of, by Captain E.M.
    Jack, 75
  man (c. 1920), *75*

Uganda. *See also* Buganda
  agriculture in, 50
  as "black" land, 63
  Britain gets control of, 60
  Christian missionaries arrive in,
    45
  climate, 38
  complications of Buganda, in, 94
  contemporary travel in, 85
  ethnic diversity of, 112
  farming, 58–59, 112
  foreign trade developed in, 57
  geography, 111
  governmental problems in,
    112–114
  Great Britain establishes pres-
    ence in, 56
  guerilla warfare in, 117
  importance of Ruwenzori range
    to, 22
  internationally recognized
    administrative divisions
    (1990), *98*
  isolation of, 30
  Jay Marston description of,
    78–79
  John Hanning Speke visits, 37
  Kampala, natives (c. 1920), *57*
  language, 112
  locally recognized administrative
    divisions (1990), *99*
  peoples of southwestern, 18
  perils of early travel in, 84
  pre-colonial, 29–31
  problems between Kenya and,
    103

religion, 112
ruler from (c. 1907–1918), *62*
wars with Tanzania, 16
wildlife in early, 38
Uganda Railway, 69
  building of, 49–50
  lion attacks on workers of, 80–81
  regions crossed by, 70
  Theodore Roosevelt's description
    of, 50–52
Ujiji
  Henry Morton Stanley finds
    David Livingstone at, 40,
    41
  Tanganyika, the market (1928),
    *41*
United Nations, 16, 63, 91, 108,
    120
  allows Italy to become trustee of
    Somali territory, 67
Uwilingiyimana, Agathe, 16

Versailles, Treaty of, 64
Victoria, Lake, 20, 48, 100, 101,
    108, 111, 126
  German rail lines reach, 50
  John Hanning Speke's descrip-
    tion of, 39
  and search for source of Nile
    River, 37
  sleeping sickness around, 81–82
  Uganda Railway reaches
    Kisumu, on, 49
Violence
  aimed at foreigners, 54
  ethnic, 15, 16, 93–94. *See also*
    Ethnic conflict
  in Kenya, 89
  in Somalia, 16, 107–108

Waboni chief and family (1905),
    *73*
Wakwavi warriors (c. 1889), *126*
Walaswanda, 39
Water commerce, 49, 50
Watussi, 76
Wazaramo, 74–75
Wildlife, 19–20, 28, 72, 100, 114,
    115
  dangers posed by, 76, 79–80
  described by Jay Marston, 78–79
  description from A.D. 916, 26–27
  description of Johann Rebmann,
    37

in early Uganda, 38
hunting of, 72–73
near Mount Kenya, 80
near Mount Kilimanjaro, 78
Serengeti, 29
specimens brought to America by
  Theodore Roosevelt, 70
stuffed, posed, *68*
in Tanganyika, 30
Theodore Roosevelt's description
  of, 52
Ugandan, described by A.F.R.
  Wollaston, 79
*William Mackinnon*, 83
Wollaston, A.F.R., 18, 21
  describes diseases in Africa,
    81–82
  describes spread of sleeping sick-
    ness, 88
  description of African in early
    1900s by, 70
  description of Ugandan wildlife
    by, 79
Woodhouse, Alfred, 73, 74
World Bank, 103
World War I, 15
  effects of, in Africa, 63
  ends German territorial rule in
    Africa, 64
World War II, 66

Young Kikuyu Association, 89

Zaire. *See* Democratic Republic of
  the Congo
  refugees of civil war flee to, 16
Zanzibar, 108. *See also* Tanganyika;
  Tanzania
  Arab influence on, 110
  arrival of Portuguese to, 34
  becomes Tanzania, 94
  British protectorate established
    on, 56
  finds humane source of income,
    35–36. *See also* Cloves
  as important trade center, 35,
    36
  independence of, 92
  racial violence on, 93–94
  sultan of (c. 1921–1927), *26*
  sultans control, 26, 34, 56
  terrible conditions on, 35
  trade between Oman and, 27

# ABOUT THE AUTHORS

**Dr. Richard E. Leakey** is a distinguished paleo-anthropologist and conservationist. He is chairman of the Wildlife Clubs of Kenya Association and the Foundation for the Research into the Origins of Man. He presented the BBC-TV series *The Making of Mankind* (1981) and wrote the accompanying book. His other publications include *People of the Lake* (1979) and *One Life* (1984). Richard Leakey, along with his famous parents, Louis and Mary, was named by *Time* magazine as one of the greatest minds of the twentieth century.

**Daniel E. Harmon** is an editor and writer living in Spartanburg, South Carolina. The author of several books on history, he has contributed historical and cultural articles to *The New York Times, Music Journal, Nautilus,* and many other periodicals. He is the associate editor of *Sandlapper: The Magazine of South Carolina* and editor of *The Lawyer's PC* newsletter.

**Deirdre Shields** is the author of many articles dealing with contemporary life in Great Britain. Her essays have appeared in *The Times, The Daily Telegraph, Harpers & Queen,* and *The Field*.